AF397622

The Renewal of Ourselves and Our World

Letters to the Friends of the Movement of Self-Knowledge

Samuel Widmer Nicolet

2024   Basic Editions · Samuel Widmer Nicolet
Switzerland
1st Edition

Layout & DTP   Romina Mossi · CH - 4574 Nennigkofen

Translation   Trevor Goode, Henning Probst, Romina Mossi,
Uma Ranganathan, Hans Frense, Jutta Frense,
Lucy Weidenbach

Original title   Die Erneuerung von uns selbst und unserer Welt,
Basic Editions 2018

Print   Book on Demand · DE · 22848 Norderstedt

ISBN   978-3-9524413-8-1

Publisher   Basic Editions
CH - 4574 Nennigkofen
E-Mail   info@basic-editions.ch
Website   https://basic-editions.ch

The Renewal of Ourselves and Our World

Letters to the Friends of the Movement of Self-Knowledge

BASIC EDITIONS

What I want

I hear the spring outside,
fresh on snow-covered meadows.
As soft rustling it comes to me,
as sunshine, and as these

early joyful first bird calls.
Glitter drunk way up there,
with heads raised up high to you,
we will reach the next goal.

.

INHALTSVERZEICHNIS

PREFACE

At the end of 2015, at a time when difficult processes and disputes related to massive stories of defamation had resulted in great uncertainty passing through the ranks of the movement that we form or to which we associate ourselves – the movement of those interested in self-knowledge – there suddenly arose in me an impulse to publish and distribute newsletters via the net. It seemed to me to make sense to strengthen in this way our inner bond. What emerged were thirty letters that define and outline our movement and summarize the basic work of self-knowledge. They also summarize in one concise work my literary activities of the past years on the subject of self-knowledge.

May it reach the hearts of many people.

Samuel Widmer Nicolet

Samuel had already prepared the preface to this book before his death in January 2017. We have therefore decided to publish it unchanged.
However, as sometimes happens in life, everything turned out differently than planned, and so we have to supplement this preface:
Samuel had planned thirty letters but only written the twenty-four published in this book. Thirteen of them appeared during his lifetime, eleven we have published with a preface after his death.
It is beautiful that we can now once again commend a book with Samuel's insights to the world.

Summer 2018

Danièle Nicolet Widmer

FOREWORD FOR THE ENGLISH EDITION

Shortly after Samuel's death, Ulrike Epping had the impulse to make Samuel's letters available to a wider audience and, together with a small group of friends, she launched a translation project. Over a period of many months, we translated as a group, exchanged ideas and struggled to find words that would convey the spirit of Samuel's writing into English as accurately as possible. The translated letters have been available to the public for a long time. We now want to bring them together in a book, as we have already done for the German version.

Our heartfelt thanks to all those who have made this book possible. Special thanks go to Trevor Goode and Henning Probst (who unfortunately is no longer with us), who accompanied me for several years in translating Samuel's texts and with whom I had the pleasure of finalising these translations. I thank them for their professionalism and passion, the exceptional quality of their work and their sensitivity to Samuel's language.

Winter 2023
Romina Mossi with Danièle Nicolet Widmer

Part I: The Movement

From this I cannot refrain,
singing to you of my affection,
whose waves beat over me,
like l'*alto mare* over a drowning man.

The ocean that overwhelms me,
is indeed the sea of love,
in which we are fused,
to a single bliss.

January 2016

Dear friends of the movement we form together

One year ago, in an unguarded moment while lying naked under the sun of the wonderful Neredu Valley in India, I predicted to my wives that the upcoming year was going to be "The Year of Decline". We had come to rest and recuperate from the efforts of the previous year (2014). A year whose summer we had named "The Tragic Summer" that followed on from 'The Magical Summer" of the year before (2013). The statement was more intended to be humorous, however, it already told of disturbing premonitions that through the experiences of the past months seemed to tarnish the view of what was to come. Though none of us would have realised, how appropriately this would finally describe the events of last year (2015).
The Year of Decline.
Slander and libel, complaints to the police, the threat of court proceedings, illnesses etc.. Not that this would have prevented us from stepping through these tests with ease and serenity. However, by the end of last year we were already taking a little more care, not wanting to recklessly expose ourselves again to what could become self-fulfilling prophecies. Despite all this, at our traditional Christmas gathering I rather presumptuously proclaimed "The Year of Promise Foretold", without quite knowing at the time exactly what had slipped out.

In the meantime, many among us have taken up this call. Everywhere there is talk about "The Year of Promise Foretold". It seems to have struck a nerve of longing that perhaps fills all of us.

Romina, who is currently occupied with the redesign of our entire internet presence, recently said that I should publish a regular newsletter on our website (https://samuel-widmer.org). After some initial hesitation, I finally heard the message and decided in future, perhaps every month, to produce a newsletter addressed to the friends of the movement we form together.

We are a movement. Similar to the way it slowly dawned on us in the *Kirschblüte* Community some fifteen years ago that we were gradually mutating into a community, we have become conscious during the last year, especially through the adversity that we had to experience, that we have in the meantime gone beyond this stage and that a movement has come into existence, which includes many people in Switzerland, Germany, and beyond Europe throughout the world.

As I outlined in my book "Psycholyse"[1], although the majority still hide their affiliation for understandable reasons, the movement actually formed itself a long time ago. An initial newsletter on the topic – though at that time I had still not quite understood it as such – had actually already been sent into the world a few months ago. I include it here again as an annex[2]. It was prompted at the time by an active member of this movement who was concerned about our further development. Of course it naturally coincided closely with "The Forbidden Path" (www.der-verbotene-weg.de), the initiative of another courageous colleague with the same concerns, who awoke in some of us the awareness of our "being on the move". This previous mail exchange can be seen very much as a prelude to the undertaking by Romina to write newsletters. Not always, but sometimes, it can take me a while before

---

[1] Samuel Widmer Nicolet: Psycholyse/ Bis dass der Tod uns scheidet.../ Psycholytische Psychotherapie/ Die Geschichte der substanzunterstützten Psychotherapie in der Schweiz und in Europa nach 1970; Basic Editions, 2013 [Until Death Separates Us.../ Psycholysis/ Psycholytic Psychotherapy/ The History of Substance Supported Psychotherapy in Switzerland and Europe after 1970]

[2] Annex 1: Exchange of e-mails between Ulrike Epping and Samuel Widmer

I understand the commission of the Great Spirit regarding the next task to which I am entrusted.
In any case, I have now understood: Here is my first newsletter addressed to the movement that we form together.

At the time, fifteen years ago, when we started to see ourselves as a community in Lüsslingen-Nennigkofen, we soon adopted a name. The *Kirschblüte Community* [The Cherry Blossom Community]. The movement we form together had already received a beautiful name, chosen many years ago by the members of the then Master Course for Psycholytic Psychotherapy. We are the WordWideMagicMovement (https://world-wide-magic-movement.org). Perhaps in the near future, my newsletters will also be found in this forum and will hopefully inspire us, should we ever become lethargic and sleepy.

What is the sense and purpose of a newsletter, I asked myself. What might this sense and purpose be in relation to a movement, our movement? Should not such a collection of writings express over time the most important and fundamental concerns of such a movement? Should not the objectives of the movement as well as the tools to achieve these objectives be described once again anew and in more detail? Are not these objectives simply the renewal of ourselves and our world, which we hope to accomplish through the tool of self-knowledge? Have we not come to make the earth a paradise? Krishnamurti was one of our most important teachers and we have benefited much from his wisdom. In a recently published new book[3] he wonderfully summarises these concerns and at the same time indicates the importance of being a light to oneself; so wonderfully that I would like to include them in the annex (annex 2).
But what does it actually mean to belong to a movement? We are in no way an organization with membership and defined obligations and rights. In my aforementioned book, "Psycholysis", I attempted to describe an open heart-community that defines itself only through bonds of friendship and a common sense of purpose. "You belong here," announces the WWMM at

---

[3] Jiddu Krishnamurti: This Light in Oneself, True Meditation. Shambhala Publications, 1999

the top of its home page and in doing so, it proclaims a membership based solely on love.

Since the prophecy of "The Year of Promise Foretold" was gladly taken up by so many people, I needed to subsequently figure out what "promise foretold" actually means and then what indeed might be promised to us.

In its origin and usage, the term "promise foretold" is associated with elevated language. It describes a prediction or even divination of the future and is predominantly positive in character. It tells of something that is promised, that has been foretold. The birth of the Messiah was in its time foretold to the Jews, and the prospect of eternal life after death was promised to the believers.

Here we are dealing with simpler more earthly matters. Actually, nobody has announced, foretold, or promised us anything. But the longing, which unites us and about which we have already spoken, perhaps works like a foretelling within us, perhaps we experience it like a promise foretold, whose fulfilment we are awaiting.

What are we longing for? What result do we expect, when we wholeheartedly follow the path of self-knowledge, when we endeavour to be sincere heart-warriors?

Communities of people, in which everyone personally knows each other, are said to be held together by the shared gossip (in the positive sense). However, gossip as glue and cement is no longer sufficient in movements that include too many people for everyone to know each other personally. Movements, connections among larger groups of people, are held together by myths, such as a shared mistaken belief in eternal growth, or the second coming of a saviour or big money, or whatever.

Is not part of our myth – the myth that fuses our WorldWideMagicMovement together – the quiet conviction that we will suffer no harm, that we will happily and untouched walk the earth as a light, commissioned to enlighten without harm being inflicted on us, that before they can reach us our enemies will be defeated by the friendly forces of the universe to whom we are committed? Ultimately, we expect that the earth, and humanity in particular, will evolve to be a haven of peace, happiness and love. Since it will obviously take a long time until this will have taken place, we hope that in the period beforehand to at least have personal protection and security, while we fulfil the task assigned to us by the Universal Spirit.

Is that what the coming year will bring? And is it merely a desperate hope that we are clinging to, nothing but an illusion, or a genuine reality that is to prevail and show itself.

We shall see. We will know in a year.

Because this is definitely another key concern of the newsletters that I intend to send: To extol the myth that holds our movement together so that it becomes and remains strong and powerful. Because we are dedicated to self-knowledge, it is our hope that this myth will illuminate reality and not represent a mere delusion. The difference is, that instead of it remaining repressed and taboo as is usual, we remain consciously aware of our myth-creation and consciously employ it as an instrument of our intention and thus escape the great danger of illusion and aberration.

Of course, it would be nice if all the difficulties that have arisen would resolve themselves in the coming year, if all the obstacles that have been placed in our way would disappear again. Hopes and wishes are, however, just as unhelpful as fears and anxieties. They all conceal the clear view of reality. Our way is to welcome good and evil alike, and to accompany both in the same manner with inner stillness. To live fully and completely with reality, that is our credo. Perhaps, in this way, we will finally go beyond all myth-making, and as its avant-garde, be allowed to lead evolution into its further unfolding as pure reality. And who knows, perhaps it is for exactly this reason, that our foretold promise is the joy and blessing of the Great. We will see.

May joy be with you.

Samuel Widmer Nicolet

Lonely beside you

I feel lonely.

Whether you come,
or go,
whether you are far away,
or there beside me,
I feel lonely.
Not loved.
I feel lonely
next to you.

Like your lover
of bygone days,
who finally had to
seek his happiness,
because he found no joy with you
– you did not notice –
I feel lonely
with you.

Annex 1:
Exchange of e-mails between Samuel Widmer and Ulrike Epping

E-mail from Ulrike Epping to Samuel Widmer

Dear Samuel,

Knowing good and well that you have a lot going on, I would anyway like to share a concern. Over the weekend we met with 12 participants of the master course. One could feel a lot of fear and an attempt was made to partially conceal this fear through ridiculing Christoph and his/our course of action. This was to be expected, yet I feel deeply affected by it. So much disunity. This fear is not only about "standing up", but also about losing you as a man, a master, a guru. I tried to talk about it and encountered a great deal of resistance.

They did not see that this movement is needed, the Movement of Love, the movement which says "I am Sam", "We are Samuel", the movement of "oneness". Of course, this clearly means to grow up, to take responsibility, to be warriors. It was good that this could become apparent.

Here is my request: Your word carries great weight and could possibly help to somewhat straighten out things. Could you very briefly share your own perception of it all with the different groups of people? It would of course be much nicer if it could be done without you. But right now that's the way it is.

Heartfelt greetings

Ulrike

E-mail from Samuel Widmer to Ulrike Epping: The vision

Dear Ulrike,

Of course, I am watching quite carefully the beginning of the movement triggered by recent events. Various initiatives have been launched and these seem likely to become more visible in the future. The action which Christoph Kahse has initiated, together with the film by Dirk Liesenfeld on psycholysis, seem to be among the strongest right now. Indeed, the two have linked up and have united with each other. This is where one can feel the most passion and involvement.

What is actually happening in terms of the moment that triggers (the difficult events) and in terms of the action (the response to these events)?
It seems obvious to me that something is trying to come to light. It needs to and wants to. For me the whole thing is a consistently positive process (even including my current tendency "to be absent and thus fall into a new sphere of activity"). It is obviously time for all that was being prepared in secret to emerge into the light. And it is not only about us and about psycholysis, but also about something much bigger that is happening in the world.
Unfortunately, this always brings an initial fear. A lot of fear. But love is the light and the fear wants to dissolve into love.

It also seems to me that we cannot avoid the likelihood that this "coming to light" will once again (as it has always done over a long time) lead to much incomprehension, to many misunderstandings and a great deal of rebellion by the forces of the old story. How else can it be when an old paradigm looks upon the emergence of a new one. Never mind. Actually, one can stay calm regarding this matter. Nothing can happen to you besides the fate which you will anyway have to meet.
What naturally comes to light initially is the cowardice, the lukewarm attitude and half-heartedness on the side of the new movement. And this is a good thing. It will separate the wheat from the chaff. And as we have already experienced, fate does not let such people go when they want to escape (especially those among them who are more mature and therefore more responsible). It is precisely such people who are dragged into the light by the process so that they can serve the cause through negativity. It will probably overtake others among the awakened and mature if they do not go along with the movement of their own accord. This movement is needed.
Observing Christoph's "campaign" for quite a while now, it surprises me that from out of nowhere there has been an outcry going through the ranks at last:

not even 200 signatures, less than 20 self-portraits! What a miserable response considering the number of people who have benefitted from the work!

Christoph will learn through all this, that in the end you are always alone and deserted, and that it is here that the greatest strength lies. And so it doesn't matter. This too is fine. But then, where are all the profiteers and scaredy-cats, where is the acknowledgement that would have hardly cost them anything. Indeed no one need confess to anything illegal when they speak out for psycholysis. We have never stood for anything illegal, only for something thoroughly legitimate.

And of course, as soon as anyone takes over the leadership in a Group of all Leaders, all the unfinished authority problems and problems of competiveness are awakened. All the envy and opposition comes to a head. In the best case, this can lead to a solution. In the worst case, it leads to the exclusion of all that does not fit. All this is good. This is what it is all about. The hour of truth!

Personally, we ourselves stand right in the midst of it all and as good stalkers we try to surf the wave of energy and to use its strength for our concerns, and in so doing we remain smart enough so that neither we nor anyone else here comes to harm. This is a great art. And whether we will succeed is a question of destiny. Accepting every conceivable fate that might follow, even possible failure, is a prerequisite for being able to shape the process without fear. Maybe we will fail, maybe we have been chosen to play the part of the last martyrs. All this depends essentially on how much power can be generated by the current movement and how the struggle between fear and love, between cowardice, envy, betrayal and sober compassion, develops in the individuals as well as in the whole group. Real power belongs to him who can stand alone in all this and in whom there is space for all possibilities and therefore all feelings. In the end, this will in any case prevail. What a great mystery play! (And just between ourselves: We will certainly not fail. Just wait and see, two or three years!)

We did not come to help psycholysis achieve a breakthrough in medical terms at the expense of its actual potential. This may, however, play a role as a side effect and we are grateful to the forces that do at least campaign for it. We ourselves have set out to bring the actual potential of this whole affair to the world, to realize the vision of evolution behind it and a victory of love over fear among human beings. Although it has always seemed hopeless and right now, seems almost impossible, we are still in good spirits. All said and done, we are backed by the very purpose of evolution.

In regard to psycholysis, this means that on the one hand it is not all that important, and on the other hand that it functions as a symbol for this fundamental issue. Therefore, we stand for the right to continue the practice of shamanism as a cultural heritage for all people. We do not accept that basic human rights, which have existed for thousands of years, be abolished and, using all means, even our lives, we stand to defend these even unto death.

As for me, I support with my goodwill any initiative in this direction and in turn feel myself supported and carried by every impulse which moves in this direction. As for the lukewarm forces of the cowards and those who merely exploit the movement or even the dark forces of the slanderers and traitors, I keep away from them and as far as possible, do not want to get entangled with them. In one way or another they always serve the Whole, everything serves the Whole, the same Whole to which I am committed, hence I neither have to fight nor condemn them. Wherever I can, I use their limited power for the cause of love. My temporary "absence" is not just a personal circumstance in an even larger dimension of this whole action that will also finally serve the whole story, but rather more than that, it awakens the dormant powers in others, whose time has come to finally grow up and emerge into the light. Surely there is something wonderful even about this. Those first steps into the loneliness of great abandonment which precedes the all-encompassing movement of love may also show some childish excesses, but so what? Do we have to be against it? Do we not want to reach the young souls as well? Why is it that when one tries to do something in the world, so many people always waste their energy in criticism, instead of doing something on their own, even if they do not wish to extend a helping hand? And why not just get whole-heartedly carried away by another person's impulse, and offer your own contribution? And why not do it with childlike zeal: I'm Sam! I am psycholysis! I am you! It's definitely better than "I am an a...! I'm an idiot! I'm a failure!", something that the eternal critics ought to perhaps for once honestly and openly admit to themselves.

In the material dimension in which we are currently at home, the struggle, the fight, has always been between fear and love, and it will also remain this way. Competition, cowardice, discord are all servants of this fear. Whoever really wants to stand in the light, as a warrior of the heart, will end this age-old battle in themselves by overcoming these "foes" through fully integrating them. Finally, he is in agreement with everything. He sees that destiny is right. He is against nothing.

I do not know, dear Ulrike, whether with my scribbling I have managed to touch the nerve which you wanted to have touched. It has not been brief, but you cannot expect brevity from me, a person predisposed to epics. In any case, thank you for the suggestion that I comment on the whole matter. It has helped me. What you could say to all and what you could spread far and wide is that: Although for many it might seem quite different and temporarily also turn out quite different, we are definitely committed to ultimately the most successful force in the universe. To the unity of all forces. To the evolution of consciousness and love. To the vision of love! And we have time. In any case we will prevail. And we are grateful that we may stand in this power, the power of love, and not starve among the shabby forces that must avoid something.

I wish that you, like Christoph, Dirk and all others, will dare to be totally consumed by this fire and not fall victim of the devil who wants to organize things. May you be granted a beautiful day full of love, a love which can carry and bear everything...

Samuel

PS: If you wish to and if it seems useful to you, you may disseminate what I write here, through all channels, but the letter should be unabridged and appear together with your own mail. Marianne will be able to assist you. Maybe it will help.

Annex 2:
The Light in Oneself, Chapter 1 – A New Consciousness – adopted from Krishnamurti's Journal

A new consciousness and a totally new morality are necessary to bring about a radical change in the present culture and social structure. This is obvious, yet the left and the right and the revolutionary seem to disregard it. Any dogma, any formula, any ideology, is part of the old consciousness; they are the fabrications of thought whose activity is fragmentation: the left, the right, the centre. This activity will inevitably lead to bloodshed of the right or of the left or to totalitarianism. This is what is going on around us. One sees the necessity of social, economic and moral change but the response is from the old consciousness thought being the principle actor. The chaos, the confusion and the misery that human beings have got into, stems from the realm of the old consciousness. Without a profound change of this consciousness, every human activity – be it political, economic or religious – will only bring us to destruction of each other and the earth. This is completely obvious to any right-minded person.

One has to be a light to oneself; this light is the law. There is no other law. All the other laws are made by thought and thus lead to separation, division and working against each other. To be a light to oneself means never following the light of another, however reasonable, logical, historically justified and convincing it may be. You cannot be a light to yourself if you are in the dark shadows of authority, of dogma, of conclusion. True morality is not put together by thought; it is not the outcome of environmental pressure, it is not of yesterday, of tradition. True morality is the child of love and love is not desire and pleasure. Sexual or sensory enjoyment is not love.

Freedom is to be a light to oneself; then it is not an abstraction, a thing conjured by thought. Actual freedom is freedom from dependency, attachment, from the craving for experience. Freedom from the very structure of thought is to be a light to oneself. In this light all action takes place and thus it is never contradictory. Contradiction exists only when that light, is separate from action, when the actor is separate from action. The ideal, the principle, is the barren movement of thought and cannot co-exist with this light; one denies the other. Where the observer is, this light, this love, is not. The structure of the observer is put together by thought, which is never new, never free. There is no "how", no system, no practice. There is only the seeing which is the doing.

You have to see, not through the eyes of another. This light, this law, is neither yours nor that of another. There is only light. This is love.

To hold your hand,
and be held by you,
that is bliss! For without
your love there is nothing,

which lets joy prevail.
That in which we unfold,
is the aura pure and fine,
of your still light

Newsletter 2:
Dreaming

February 2016

Dear friends of the one path,

Before we can turn in my newsletters to the most important and fundamental concerns of the movement which we form together, as announced
in our first letter, we would like to honour in this second letter a great support which can best hold together and nourish such a movement, *dreaming*.
Dreaming, as described by Castaneda's Don Juan Matus.
In Castaneda or rather his teacher Don Juan, we have found, next to Krishnamurti, another important teacher who has contributed towards the forming
of intelligence in humanity as no other has done. Along with his comrades
he found a language suitable to describe the unknown and the unknowable;
realms that will only open up to humanity as a whole in the distant future.
"Could there be life in the universe – light years away from us – which may
also be intelligent?" An astrophysicist was recently asked in a radio interview.
The interviewer was left somewhat perplexed when she replied sceptically:
"Is there already intelligent life among us, then?"
Life itself is obviously highly intelligent and wonderful in its self-organiza-
tional unfolding, but mankind is actually not (not yet?): This is what – I
suppose – the reflective scientist wanted to express. Now as ever, Homo
sapiens refuses to use his brain in an intelligent way and thus honour to his
name. He does not want to open himself to the unfathomable intelligence
of the universe.

Dreaming is a way to open up to the unfathomable. It has only a limited association with normal dreaming and is much more an immersion into an inner spiritual reality which has been enclosed in a material realm. In no way does it rival the coarsely structured material reality. On the contrary, it encompasses it, even giving birth to it, and actually by far exceeding it in terms of real content. Whoever wants to look at it more closely can read about it in the books of Carlos Castaneda, which in the meantime have been ostracized by the scientific community! The small poetic text taken from my novel about community, "kirschbaumblütenblätterweiss"[4], which I recently came across again and have included as an attachment (Annex 1), may also explain something of the basic meaning behind dreaming, but which I will not go into at this point.

Dreaming is the ideal tool to unite people in a spiritual movement. This is one aspect of the significance of dreaming, as we shall see, where dreaming and stalking meet intimately. *Dreaming*, however, far surpasses the myth-making that generally holds together human movements of more than two hundred people, and moreover, it assists in the formation and establishment of the kind of mythos that actually welds people together. So indeed, it promotes the creation of the sort of myth-making which unifies large movements, but it goes even beyond that. It helps to establish the mythos of unity, which is at the bottom of all unified being, but which is ultimately the same as the actual space of Oneness. Thus *dreaming* protects against the evocation of illusionary and sentimental myths, as we have already mentioned in the first newsletter. The mythos that it produces is an accurate description of sober reality.

For years we have been training in this type of dreaming together and we send out regular invitations, to connect spiritually in this way. In the *Kirschblüte* Community we change our focus every few years by alternately turning more intensively to either the "Tantric path" or the "Art of *Dreaming*". In this way we manage to stop ourselves from becoming either completely entangled in dealing with relationships, or losing ourselves in esoteric aloofness. Mean-

---

[4] Paul Nicolet: kirschbaumblütenblätterweiss/ die ganz, ganz neue Geschichte; Basic Editions, 1999 [cherrytreeblossompetalwhite/ the completely new story]

while, each Tuesday night we offer to meet in the *dream* realm. This invitation has been open for years and will continue into the future. At least once a week we find ourselves in this inner space of Oneness with people from all over the world. The effort of the many individuals engaged in it over the course of time, is what primarily makes up our movement and represents its power. Anyone seriously engaged in it strengthens our intention and effect in the world.

Personally, I remain the stalker even in the *dream* state. For the heart warriors of Don Juan, stalking – which I will not go into at the moment – was another important art and life strategy. If you are interested, read the books by Castaneda! Stalking is only important here in this context as a means of making visible the myth-making that sets movements in motion and comes from *dreaming*. Each of us is called mainly to one or the other task provided one opens up for these things, that is, to *dreaming* or stalking.

I myself am a stalker. Even in the *dream* world, I remain a stalker. For this reason, I find that my task in the *dream* world, for example, is to prepare for the future of our movement, to dream it. The invitation to venture out into the unknown and explore the new territory of the *dream* realm, only reaches me occasionally; mainly I inspire future developments, give birth to tantric visions and strengthen the intention of the community in that I *dream* it.

Anyone, who feels connected to our movement, may at any time engage in this *dreaming*, if he wants to, and thus contribute to strengthening our cause. It does not necessarily involve much theoretical knowledge or other skills. To open up to it is enough for now. The rest will follow. Instructions come from the serious effort, from the *dreaming* itself. Experienced *dreamers* also make leaders and pick up willing beginners. Besides the exploration of infinity and all the implications that follow – which among others, impact our everyday reality – this is the task of the *dreamer* among *dreamers* in this field. Here, however, I just wanted to elaborate the relationship between *dreaming* and stalking and their joint impact on our myth-making and thus on the inner connection of spiritual movements.

What I am telling here may sound mysterious. However, we need to counter this with the fact that we are at home in a very magical and mysterious world. Only the restrictions we collectively impose upon ourselves, which then suppress us and prevent the flow of the universal intelligence in us, make us perceive the world as banal and reduced to our everyday needs. As others before us have already proclaimed, there is in fact more between heaven and earth than we dare dream of. Life is in fact infinitely more comprehensive and richer than we, with our concern for survival and our little fears about relationships, want to see. As long as we do not open up to it, the unknown and the language that tries to extol it sound mysterious to us.

What then is the future we intend, for whom do we want to *dream* the *dream?* Regarding the community movement we have called it the "new story", with regard to the tantric vision we have termed it "love in the field". In the spiritual realm we speak of the Innermost.

The intention is ultimately always directed towards the development of the Whole, to the needs of humanity, even though it will always be first visible in one's own life, one's own group. It remains the warrior's most sacred intention to overcome all division and to unify all forces, or rather to bring forth the fundamental unity of all in the deep. When it comes to the community of the warriors of the heart to which one personally belongs in terms of daily life, we have therefore spoken of the "heart group" or warrior troop: a group of people[5] deeply committed and sworn to one another and yet in no way exclusive or isolated outwardly, rather the contrary, a group that remains always focused on the connection with the universal or evolutionary intention and task.

What is then the purpose of such a focus on wholeness, on the Great?

"You have no idea how happy one can be," are words that recently slipped out of me in a small therapy group. Happiness remains the desirable goal at all levels. It is, however, another kind of happiness than the one that results from the pursuit of pleasure to which the whole of misguided humanity is committed. A happiness born of unbreakable, limitless, uncontrolled – not controlled by anything – love. A happiness that does not exclude total responsibility for everything, that is ready at all times to share the burden of another, to recognize the burden of fate.

Addiction to pleasure is seeking something completely different. It corresponds to the tainted, corrupted, comfort-loving mentality of a mankind

---

[5] A small community of less than a hundred and fifty people, normally mainly kept together by rumours as outlined in the first letter.

that has lost contact with the truth and intelligence of the Universal Spirit and pursues instead a happiness, split off from the misery that results from it. A happiness that cannot be called happiness, which is a cheap substitute for real happiness, an addiction really, which reflects the dependency of the human spirit entangled therein.

Only those who can stand alone will find access to the deep and genuine happiness that always goes together with perfect and all-embracing compassion. Those looking for pleasure split off from the whole, will never come into contact with true happiness. Such a person simply has no idea about it.

In the state of *dreaming*, in this state of pure energetic being, which can only be experienced by an energy that has completely freed itself from all states of bondage, from all conditioning, is true happiness the predominant and all-pervading feeling of life. *Dreaming* is the entry into this world of the quantum level, an internal refinement that temporarily relieves one of the world of matter and its physical laws. Not in the sense of being split off from it, the way an addict attempts to do in his search for happiness, but rather in the form of a penetration of the Innermost that overcomes and temporarily overrides the laws of the material realm. In awakening to the Innermost - that which precedes travel into the dream world one has not escaped from the coarser level of material reality and its laws into a separated spiritual realm. Rather, the former constitutes the innermost, sublime reality of this coarse material dimension. Today, quantum physics provides a useful image to understand and explain this penetration. But this can only be experienced by a mind that has itself become so subtle through the process of self-knowledge and meditation, that it becomes identical with this Innermost, highest vibration of everything. That is why the inner eye opens up to such a person. He awakes into a space of the purely spiritual.

In this innermost space the *dreamer* among *dreamers dreams* himself to the most remote places of the universe and of history, the past, while the stalker amongst the dreamers tries to guess at the future of the Whole, to fathom the intent and purpose of evolution, the universal unfolding, in order to synchronise with it.

Since the concrete, the everyday, the material is not separate from the Innermost, the quantum level – but is instead its unfolding – the stalker among *dreamers* also creates a concrete intention for his personal life and the daily life of his troop. He returns from his journey into the Innermost with knowledge; an insight and a notion which form a mission in him, a mission to materialise in the realm of everyday perception, the vision of this Innermost, the vision of an earth blossoming in love, a Whole awakened in happiness. Love is the materialization in the material world of the vision of the Innermost.

Of course, as these explanations show, dreaming also belongs to the basic and most important concerns of our movement, which we want to cover in coming newsletters. In the next newsletters, we want to look at the goals of such a movement, which we have already touched on, and the tools used to achieve these goals, the prospect of which we have already seen with dreaming and stalking.

May happiness be with you

Samuel Widmer Nicolet

Let the thinking be wordless,
a shared looking,
on which can be built
a new world.

No one need guide it!
Like nature can give,
we too want to trust,
that which holds all.

Annex:
About *dreaming,* Excerpt from the novel "kirschbaumblütenblätterweiss" [cherryblossompetalwhite] by Paul Nicolet (Pages 268-270)

She had come to learn about what still lay in the dark, now, about the world of Celia, the world of dreaming.

Dreaming was the immersion in the space of the limitless, which alone is real, the crossing of all apparent boundaries, of which the incest taboo, the border with regard to the categories of relatedness, is only the first. Crossing all the boundaries of perception so that reality can again be a single field of energy. Dreaming was having insight into the fact that there is only one reality, not two, no other, that this reality, however, contains dimensions of depth enfolded within each other, a depth which in turn knows no boundaries. It was about the transcending of all boundaries, into the space of the unthinkable, the boundary of what is material, above all to drop our idea that there is a boundary between matter and energy. To see that energy indeed materializes because it is helpful for certain purposes, that this also brings about a reality of limitation, in which there seem to be boundaries between energy and matter, but that the dimension of pure energy remains intact, remains nested, enfolded therein, can be seen and experienced at any time, that the sensation of the boundaries that go along with the material ultimately springs from a limited view, in which we need not fixate ourselves. To see that an infinite space of absolute freedom lies before us, that we can move in it all the time, that we can travel in it, in every imaginable direction, at any time, and that the door to it is not really closed. Barricaded only by our ideas, concepts, imagination, ideas about space, time and matter. That lifting the conditioning of these ideas in your own brain can push open this gate at any time.

Dreaming involved all that. Dreaming was the new story, the innermost wreath of blossoms of the flower, which forms the completely new story, the story that nobody dares to think of, no one is able to think of. The inside of a Calla blossom waiting for its awakening in the deep violet darkness under its leaves. The story we are meant for, and always have been, that is our heritage we have never stepped into, the history of paradise.

Dreaming was the crossing of the borders to the unthinkable. In it was the transcending of the incest borderline into a relationship that no longer distinguishes between mothers and sons, daughters and fathers, in which only human existence is valid, only the first step, doing away with the fundamental boundary in the dimension of pelvic energy, at the simplest, most childlike level in us.

Dreaming was the entry into the space of the infinite, the space of total freedom, the indivisible one energy.

Dreaming was travelling in it, an invitation to an infinite flight into infinite worlds, which are all completely enfolded within the one world, here right now. Here, dreaming joined up with the other discipline practiced by people of the new story, stalking. The training of the ability to exist completely unnoticed in the world of mediocrity, as a free-flying dreamer, unnoticed, as long as you wanted it so. Undetected.

Dreaming was the giving up of every restriction. Stalking was the ability to be invisible in it. Unless you had your reasons. Like Sebastian. Who had gone to jail. Because he was called upon to thus break a wall.

There is only one reality. To be in it is a journey without end into unlimited depths. Not being in it is our reality, the normal, the imprisonment in notions that human thinking has invented over reality. To be thought, instead of reality. To be thought instead of energy. To be thought instead of perception. To be thought instead of love. Two completely different states that do not touch each other. The one: thought, fear, that is the old story. It has no relation to the new, to the other state. Love, perception without limit: that is the other state, the one feeling, the new story. It encloses within itself the old one, which cannot have any relation to it. Being thought instead of love. Being shadow, like most people. A shadow of one's own possibilities. Something unreal. This reality of thinking has a thousand different spaces, many realities. But they are all not real. They are all made of the same stuff, of thought energy. A self-contained space. Without any contact with the vast space of the real.

In the realm of real reality, all the energy of the thought-world, out of which the whole, infinite suffering of humanity, the endless stream of human consciousness is constructed, is only a point. A small point.

At first, Ramilah's understanding of all this was vague. Her consciousness had started to open to something else being there, which she did not know. The gate began to open. As always, when the brain becomes silent in the knowledge of its not-knowing, it becomes receptive. That's why she came

back. That's why she wanted to help further carry the materialization of the new story that had begun here. That's why she wanted to learn in the pressure cooker that Sebastian had created here; that's why she wanted to let Celia introduce her to the secrets of the night. Into the heart of the calla blossom, to Sebastian, who was waiting there for her.
Sebastian?
But had he not died long ago? Or was he there? Waiting inside the calla blossom for the unfolding of the vibrations of her perception? Would he be her teacher? Pulling from the other side, while Celia and her helpers would push her from this side.

This side was calling her. Ramilah woke up from her weightless flights. She got up and headed off. To Tanita and Phillip, her father, who was not her father at all. This side surrounded her as she put her clothes back on and looked around, the absolute, sensual, one reality that Sebastian had loved so much. Which Sebastian loved so much?
The reality of the body, of the senses, of the pelvis, of which everything beyond, all that is sacred, all that is transcendental is not separate, but rather enfolded therein. One thing.
A swarm of mosquitoes were dancing over the pond. Dragonflies hovering over the dark water. The water lily pads stood closely packed at the other end of the pool, reflecting the darkening sky. And crickets were chirping around. The frogs, which had settled here, were croaking, and the birds, with their clamouring cries were searching for their sleeping places in the hedges. There was a shine, a glow, over all this. The cherry tree stood there, huge and with its strong arms embraced the rich violet shadows. The birches swayed and whispered. Ramilah remained there for a moment, in total perception, totally that, totally this dance of union, the infinite movement of the One, which is constantly seeking itself, connecting itself with itself to, again and again, give birth anew. She was completely silent, so she received the stillness out of which all dance is an expression; and in this stillness, a wide gate opened into the Infinite.

To me, you are devoted,
at your feet I lie down,
my incredulity, you diamond,
you unhoped-for joy.

On harsh paths of destiny
living the unheard-of;
in thorn hedges, see, there hides
the rose that I pick!

March 2016

Dear friend of the great movement of life,

With what are you occupied right now, at this moment? Do you ever wonder about this in the midst of the turmoil of your life? And what do you see? What do you recognize? What is your honest answer? Are you driven by fear, ambition or envy? Do you find yourself entangled in conflict? Are you full of defence, controlling and intellectualizing?

Or are you at the moment taken up by love, embraced by love? Does one find you loving, do you find yourself loving, in every moment of life, whenever you stop for a while and ask yourself this question? Or are you at the moment occupied with something else?

Self-knowledge.

A good means to self-knowledge is every now and then to halt and confront such a question.

If you can answer this question every time with a yes, then you are probably a fully awakened Tantrika, a fully awakened person. Then you are probably truly fully aware of the great movement of life, of love, belonging to the Whole. Then you are ahead of others.

Do you, at least from time to time, ask yourself these or similar questions? If so, you could perhaps count yourself among those who are awakening, among the serious seekers with regard to self-knowledge. If on the other hand such questions are entirely alien to you, then you are probably sleeping the deep sleep of the unconscious.

Self-knowledge, the tool of the movement by means of which we hope to renew ourselves and our world.

Like everything else we are a part of the great movement of life, of love, of the Whole. And this expresses itself in our daily lives through the fact that we count ourselves as part of the movement and among those interested in the use of psychotherapy, community-making, psycholysis and Tantra as means of support. But the core of these disciplines is self-knowledge. As outlined in our first newsletter regarding the formulation of the most important and fundamental concerns of such a movement, self-knowledge, about which we shall talk later, is one of the main tools for achieving the goals of our movement.

Self-knowledge, honest examination of one's motives, observation of all one's actions and thoughts in the current moment, is the alpha and omega of awakening. Accurate self-knowledge, which does not indulge in any illusions, euphemisms or justifying explanations. Which sticks unconditionally to the facts, to that which is.

Lately, and increasingly often, I have noticed how the people we have accompanied for many years and who have already gone far on the path of self-discovery and awakening, have never fully resolved their dependency on the student-teacher relationship because they have never become completely independent in terms of accurate self-examination. Even after years, they still need an impetus, a confrontation, in order to be really honest with themselves and not to pretend in certain situations. It is not that they would like to keep experiencing the state of a student, who must be admonished. On the contrary, they are longing for equality, longing to be at the same level as the teacher, to be free of authority, to stand alone in the field of love. But they do not summon up the necessary accuracy and honesty, even after years. Due to their lack of accuracy, they create an authority, the teacher-student gap, against which they then have to rebel, again and again.

What might be the reason? What prevents them from questioning themselves at any time, from understanding what is happening? Why are they themselves not a light?

Are they not serious enough? Do they shy away from independence, from standing alone?

The ability for true self-examination brings all dependency in internal matters to an end: dependency on therapy and spiritual support, dependency on authority. It awakens its own illumination, brings clarity and truth. No one else needs to push them any more into seeing what is.

Real self-knowledge unerringly confronts one with the inner reality of one's life at every moment; it closely monitors one's own behaviour in relationships. No thought, no secret motive, no sneaky calculation escapes it. It sees everything as it is, without condemning, without judging, without comparing. It simply sees. And with what it sees, it does nothing. It is enough to look. Because in this pure act of looking and seeing, the observer and what is observed come together. And thus each division has its end. Wholeness is found. This leads to the miracle of transformation. To this wonderful alchemical transformation that takes place in oneself, in which lead turns into gold as soon as one faces reality. That which is, comes to an end. And something else starts to shine through. The lead, the heaviness of unconsciousness, gives way to the ease of a fully expanded awareness. That which is, cannot be improved, nor be changed. It is. But in the honest admission of its existence, it comes to an end. It dissolves. The spirit which has become whole, in which every division has ceased, goes beyond, all by itself. In the next newsletter we will consider which gate thus opens and into which dimension the mind awakens at this point. At this point let us merely say: Through precise knowledge of the self, self-knowledge eventually leads to its own end and to the end of the self that it has been observing. Something new begins at this point. Love takes the lead.

Freedom is important. There must be no authority in the field of self-knowledge. As long as we remain dependent on guidance for self-knowledge, dependent on psychotherapy, this can never come about completely. People, who remain dependent in this sense, cannot spearhead the movement of the Whole. Any movement that they establish remains weak. They cannot really stand up for themselves and for the movement they created. They cannot stand alone. In the realm of self-knowledge, one must ultimately go it completely alone. A strong movement arises when the individual exponents can stand alone. It is self-organising through standing alone. There is nothing else one needs to do. Their love brings forth the true movement, once the individuals standing alone are aligned at the same time, with the same intensity and passion, with the same intention. Then miracles take place. Real movement cannot be based upon dependency, organized togetherness, or suchlike. Its basis must be aloneness and real relationship. It must be based on love.

But what is real relationship? Time and again there is confusion. In a real relationship there are ultimately no dependencies, in the sense of not being fully self-reliant. At the same time real relationship, love, does not shy away from dependency in any way.

It is good every now and then to confront the issue of ties and dependency. Thinking that one cannot live without another is indeed unhealthy; it makes one dependent and has a lot to do with fear and little to do with love. However, without this feeling that a life without the other is meaningless, one is missing the spice of life and is left not really knowing personal love. For those who do not surrender to this feeling, all relatedness remains stale and meaningless. People who cringe away from it are not able to form a sustaining movement.

Is it a question of degree? I do not think so. Even though this may play a role and even though pathological clinging will destroy any togetherness, the joy of love rest above all else on the totality of surrender and falling for each other.

Neediness, especially neediness in regard to love, is obviously not love, but merely dependence. But to want others, to need each other is not wrong. Rather, it is natural. Whoever is afraid of it, whoever needs to ward it off, will not be able to open himself to a great life, to a field of love. No world-changing movement will come from him. On the other hand, it would actually testify to a lack of independence, of being trapped by childish or pathological demands, if you were not able to sustain a loss without sinking. A healthy, strong person, capable of loving, will be involved in a variety of dependencies, but he will also know how to rebalance them, as soon as there is a leak at any point.

A loving person, a person who has gone to the end of the process of self-knowledge until the dissolution of the self, will be occupied above all else with loving. Precisely because he realises that an existence without commitments loses its meaning, he will serve the needs of others over an extensive range. He will be reliable in mutual agreements, unhesitatingly accompany children into adulthood and willingly carry those who are dependent, wherever he is called to do so. He will also be able to allow himself to be loved and supported, when he needs it. When this is so, dependence is not a problem, rather it happens as a matter of course. Nevertheless, it is true that it has nothing to do with love. A healthy human being will not mistake things or bring about confusion. He can deal with these dynamics, knows his needs and is not inhibited about taking what he requires. Mostly, however, he will be occupied with love, which means to care. Taking care of the needs of others and especially of the Whole.

When you come across awakened human beings you will find them engaged in loving at every moment of their lives. People who have seriously become involved with the path of self-knowledge are always, everywhere, and in any situation, occupied with loving. Whatever else there is to be done, their main focus is on loving. Our movement is concerned with psycholysis, Tantra and community-making, because they can support self-knowledge and therefore loving. Together we form a movement that raises self-knowledge into the central theme of our lives. But self-knowledge flows into love; that is why we see ourselves as a movement of loving.

Dear friend of the great movement of life and of the movement that we form together, with what are you occupied, now, at this moment? Are you able to even perceive that? Are your senses, your power of observation, your awareness sharpened enough that you can see it? Are you, as a mature Tantrika, aware of each blink of the eye?

May happiness be with you

Samuel Widmer Nicolet

PS: Many have been asking me about the situation now concerning the legal notification made against us a year ago in March 2015. Therefore a few words of clarification. The notification led to the initiation of a criminal investigation. This continues, although the investigations have failed to produce any results which would have justified an indictment. As the entire procedure seemed to me to be so lacking in any relationship, I decided to occasionally (every three months) write a personal letter to the chief prosecutor. I am attaching the first of these letters from June 2015.

Annex: Letter to the prosecutor of June 2015 including the article by Bogenberger and the prosecutor's answer

What is your fortune, what is mine?
Do you hear how it whispers above,
do you note how it rustles below,
do you see its turbid gaze?

Do you know my role, your role,
the one you play in this round dance,
the one, without diversion,
I here should willingly give?

A kiss of tired fate,
scream of mankind, not to envy,
throws us into a silent suffering,
a penance imposed by gods.

2nd June 2015

Department of Public Prosecution
For the attention of Mr Claudio Ravicini
Franziskanerhof
Barfüssergasse 28
P.O. Box 157

4502 Solothurn

Personal questions

Dear Mr Ravicini,

I have not been familiar with matters relating to a criminal investigation up to now and am only gradually learning what is to be expected. Mainly stress, this much I have already understood! However, it has surprised me that we have not spoken again since the beginning of the matter almost three months ago. I thought, therefore, that I would just contact you on my own initiative.

What amazes me about the whole story is why we cause each other so much mutual stress. I probably rightly assume that this causes as much of a headache for you, as it does for me and for us. But I can see even our lawyers wriggling on the hook of excessive demands, and it is likely that the accusers, Ms. Bundschu and Ms. Bogensberger, are now equally plagued by the challenges that they themselves have unleashed.
"I am just doing my job," you repeatedly assured me during our first and only conversation which was incidentally very pleasant.
I am doing exactly the same thing as well: I am doing my job. And I am doing it conscientiously and well, as brought home by the accompanying article, which Ms. Bogenberger wrote as a press release a few years ago.

That is why I am surprised. I see that we are committed to the same thing, to a better world. To a healthier and more orderly world. We can hardly heal it with this stress. This is why I am surprised.

What I would much rather suggest to you is: "Why not rather take a walk with our children in the forest?" I suppose you also have children. Or even grandchildren? And as I perceived you, I assume that you love them as much as I do mine and ours.

To propose something like this (or generally anything) would however be presumptuous; hence I prefer to let it be. But it really would be worth considering, whether we could not thus bring more happiness into all our lives.

Ms. Bogenberger wrote the accompanying article a few years ago (9 Dec. 2008) entirely voluntarily and without being asked, as even then waves of misconceptions and slander had been already rising high. I found it by chance during the laborious survey of our computer files relating to patient data that needed to remain sealed because of medical confidentiality. These are things you will find and that will make life more difficult for you, if the custodial judge or, should the need arise, the Federal Court give the green light for it.

Even Ms. Bogenberger and Ms. Bundschu may count on my protection for as long as I have not been exempted from my duty of confidentiality. To free myself from it, would only make sense if the stress were to continue. However, it seems to me that I can release this article – Mrs Bogenberger also sees herself as a journalist – as it was made available for public release. It actually sums up quite well what I wanted to tell you: That we are really engaged in the same thing, in the service for a better, more orderly and healthy world. And that I do my job well. It could stand for that which Mrs Bogenberger no longer wanted to stand for in the end (when she withdrew her willingness to testify.) Is it not amazing how perspectives and "truths" can change?

You are right: We are only doing our job.

Although I will probably not have much to say in this whole affair, may I permit myself to ask the following question: Do we not prefer to support each other in our effort towards a healthier system, instead of competing against each other? Would it not make more sense, for all the forces which want good, to unite rather than become mired in conflict with each other? Is it really unavoidable that the vindictive story of bullying which has been pursuing me and our efforts for years, must now also be fought out at this level?

I am not complaining. And I will appear without grudge, if it really is required. It is not that I fear a fight. But I did not want to refrain from asking.

I hope you do not take negatively my presumption in having contacted you directly. I do not mean to offend you in any way. And neither to influence you in any way. In this respect, you would have misunderstood me. On the contrary, I dare to make this overture because I have perceived your humanness and integrity. And maybe I also find it encouraging that in another case to do with a tax matter (also related to a story concerned with years of bullying) a personal letter to the President of the Federal Court surprisingly found a hearing. It helped me to restore my belief in the rationality of our legal and political system, which was rather tarnished at that time.
I do not actually expect anything from you either. It has just been an occasion for me to express something from the heart. After all, we are just doing our jobs. And I do believe that you do yours as diligently as I do mine.

I thank you for having listened to me and send you friendly greetings.

Dr. med. P. Samuel Widmer Nicolet

Annex: A news article published by Ariela Bogenberger on 9 Dec. 2008

If it were really so …
(An article, press release, supporting arguments etc.)

I have now known the psychiatrist Samuel Widmer and his wife Danièle Nicolet for almost 10 years. On my last visit to Switzerland, I was very surprised by the excited media coverage. I am now supposed to have landed up with a drug and sex guru?

The less than perfect side of me thinks: If it really were so…! Gurus, so I hear, require that you turn in your common sense at the door – as a ticket to a blessed world in which one hands over one's own responsibility to the master. If you follow the fantasy of my journalist colleagues, an image arises of enslaved disciples who, having been brainwashed, mate wildly at the feet of the Master. Now unfortunately, the reality is very different. You can believe me, because I have visited a great many workshops and unlike the reporters, have accurately read some of Widmer's books.

I have experienced Samuel Widmer as a human being and a teacher – by the way, I don't have a problem at all with this term – who applies high ethical standards first and foremost to himself. It was only through his example and his gentle accompaniment that I learned to take responsibility for myself in an irresponsible world. Also in regard to sexuality! "First comes love, then sex" I heard him often say. While married, he fell in love. Like most honourable people he could have hidden his mistress in an apartment in the city, to visit her secretly. That would have probably spared him a lot of trouble. But Widmer, precisely because he all is about love, consequently gave his beloved a place in his life and at his side. Personally, I see him more as being a conservative in the best sense of the word. And his private life is actually none of our business, right? Neither is whatever happens in the bedrooms of the community in Lüsslingen.

Samuel Widmer steadfastly follows his own values. Especially his dream of the blossoming of love among human beings. In this regard, one should also look at his work and his life. Well, so there is someone who thinks we humans could lead more honest, better and loving lives together, if we listened to the voice of love and followed it wherever and however it manifests itself in our lives. That's what he tries to do – steadfastly and unswervingly. And that is also what makes him seem exotic in the eyes of the common man.

What do drugs now have to do with all of this?

For thousands of years people have been using certain aids to fathom the meaning of their existence. Of course, also to make this earthly life more bearable. Think of all the people for whom the rigors of our fast-paced world are lightened by their daily wine or beer? Today a huge pharmaceutical industry makes a turn-over of billions with psychotropic drugs. Thousands of resources have been researched and produced to calm people, stimulate them, to make them happy or to tear them out of the depths of depression. Now, Samuel Widmer makes use of legal substances as a means of support in psychotherapy to help people to better understand themselves. The report implies, that this is about the excessive use of intoxicating substances by irresponsible addicts. Here too I must unfortunately disappoint you: what is practiced is respectful, quiet and disciplined self-examination, during which, in all these years, I have neither experienced nor observed a single instance of encroachment. In a sheltered environment we track down difficult feelings, whose discovery is a foundation on the path of psychological healing and self-exploration. Interestingly, the work with these substances often leads to fast and lasting success in the area of addiction.

Now I come to what I think is the problematic part, the accusations about incest. This is probably the biggest misconception that has arisen about Samuel Widmer. Although it is not directly said in the press, it is suggested: Widmer feels that sex with minors is good and possibly practices it. Such an accusation alone, even if it is unfounded, can damage the reputation of a person on a long-term basis. Therefore one should exercise great care and please do careful research.

This is exactly what Samuel Widmer does not do!

He is concerned with the impact of the fear of incest in the relations between people. If you follow his admittedly surprising theses, one encounters an issue of cultural-historical significance. Similar to the discoveries of Freud or perhaps Darwin that are still denied today and regarded with hostility in parts of the world.

Here Samuel Widmer proceeds from a premise that I have to admit one can understand very little theoretically. You have to experience it yourself: Love that is! He regards it as the fundamental force that connects us people together in the heart. Indeed, he stands for the best Western tradition of Christian world exploration, in which spirituality and science were by no means separated. If one follows him in this assumption, it makes many things more clear. Although of course the term "respectable" incest is a problematic concept for me too: As mother of three children, it brings up for me, the same fear of the likelihood of injury or violent assault as it probably does with every reader who is confronted with it for the first time. But yes, that's exactly the point. It is about the fear of incest. It is precisely this fear of incest that has led people to develop the system of order in our relations that Widmer has investigated more closely. Everyone, who himself once was in love, who loves his children, his parents, knows that love is one of the most effective, if not the most powerful force in our lives. Its expression is compassion. Widmer wondered why we humans cannot really love one another. Like one big family on one of many planets. Why do we want to make war on each other and to dominate each other? We've probably all asked this, ourselves. As I understand Samuel Widmer, we human beings in the course of our evolution have replaced the bond which originally united us with nature with our systems of social order. But love is actually the basic energy that connects us to a collective intelligent organism that is logically much more intelligent than us individuals. This intelligent power – also called God, Tao and many other names – would, if it could flow freely through our hearts, guide and manage our development and our lives together, always in relation to the welfare of the whole organism. But we humans have limited the free flow of love and assigned it in portions to categories associated with romance, the family and sexuality. We have tamed and channelled it, so robbing ourselves of the most fundamental force that connects us all. Thus it happens that we no longer experience ourselves as one single being, but as being separate. This goes with our inclination to define ourselves and others primarily through our roles in the world rather than through us as human beings: We are teacher, pupil, daughter, father, boss, subordinate, poor, rich, black, white, male, female. Modern man experiences himself as individual, as separate from others, unlike some primitive peoples, where this separation is not so developed.

If, for example, two people fall in love, their origin, race, religion do not matter at the emotional level. The kind of energy which two people in love can liberate, we all know. A grown up conscious human being does not need roles. He recognizes the fact that he is a human being and is there to love his fellow human. As a conscious person, one could also say awakened person, he can dispense with attributes, roles, titles and so on. He experiences "religio" – the re-connection with the Whole. When two such persons meet they are free, free to love one another, and because they are connected to the Whole, they would not harm the Whole. This means that roles no longer have any real significance. To give a sensitive and specific example: If a client is healed and has become truly free, he feels exactly which path is indicated by the home in his heart and thus the home in the Whole that he has recently found again. Seen in this light, the previously experienced division of roles – client and therapist – no longer plays a serious part, because two beings of the very same organism encounter each other. As such, it is the destiny of each being to love all beings, which would also result in the disappearing of all claims of possession in human relationships. This might sound crazy. But doesn't this view bring forth a hidden melody?

So much for the background of the incest taboo, as Widmer calls it.

Apart from that, when one looks at incest in families, at violence and rape, then there is always at the bottom of the sad story a deep despair, which comes from a lack of love. This lack leads some humans to be violent and cross boundaries. Ultimately, it finds its expression in a perverse form of sexuality. We always avoid healing and intimate closeness on the same grounds: The root fear of incest and of the disruption of the human order of relationship. What remains is a cool form of sexuality and an enormous lack of warmth in the world. By the way, Widmer understands sexuality as one possible expression of love among many others. Nowadays sexuality is anyhow mostly confused with love, which lands young people in particular often in difficulties. There is also the romanticising thought that closeness can be fulfilled with only one and not with several people. Not to speak of the devastating effect of the fear of abuse on the parent's part. Because of these reasons our sexualized world hungers for erotic scandals, for example around a sex guru! I would like to state here again that in my own experience during the whole time which I spent with Samuel Widmer, I never experienced any encroachment, not once. On the contrary, his deeply sympathetic work and his expertise as a psychiatrist has often healed traumatized victims of incest. As an artist, I know how many artists who opened up new perspectives to us were misunderstood and sometimes persecuted during their lifetime. Widmer is a progressive thinker and every now and then what he says is not easy to digest. Some of this is not at all suitable for the media to work on in a piecemeal manner. He is a researcher and boldly dares to tread on difficult new ground. Accompanied by friends, who want to practically test out a peaceful conflict-free way of living together in the form of a laboratory experiment. What is wrong with this? We do not have to go join them ourselves. We should first of all wait and see patiently whether or not we can all benefit from this daring enterprise. No, dear colleagues from the media, I have not landed up with a drug and sex guru. Not in a sect either! Rather, I have found a paternal friend, deeply concerned about human beings and the world, whose integrity I would vouch for by putting my hand in the fire at any time.

Ariela Bogenberger
(if it's useful: screenwriter, winner of the gold Grimme Prize, journalist and mother)

A spring day shines in new splendour,
first snowdrops already taking form;
morning joy never heeds the clock,
it entrusts itself and surrenders to its dance.

It seems the miracle has chosen me.
As if I had not already lost everything,
it protects me who stumbles in utter darkness,
like a warm mantle or canopy,

the me, so long now without all honour,
beholding mutely the young light in all,
grasping astonished the deepmost there,
drawing from its bright still magic.

Public Prosecutor

Franziskanerhof
Barfüssergasse 28, Postfach 157
4502 Solothurn
Telefon 032 627 60 40
Telefax 032 627 60 41

Mr
Paul Samuel Widmer Nicolet
Rebe 138
4574 Nennigkofen

9th June 2015

Dear Dr. Widmer

Thank you for your letter "Personal questions" of 2 June 2015. You will surely understand that in my role of lead prosecutor in the enquiry conducted against you, I will not be able to answer the - certainly interesting - questions you have posed.

I kindly request you to please take note of this.

Yours sincerely
The prosecutor

C. Ravicini

To be send to
Paul Samuel Widmer Nicolet, Rebe 138, 4574 Nennigkofen, by priority mail

Case number **STA 2015.740** */SCR*   02099686.doc
Please always indicate

I see you, gracious,
before the sun, pale and heavy
from winter's scourge,
seeping over me anew
in the glory of pre-spring
early blossom. And from where
and how comes this foreboding of
momentous rebuke?

Let us thus make nimble
and soon find our happy end,
and through love great and dense
eschew the bygones of the past,
honour what sprang forth anew,
raise ourselves into pure light,
celebrate what never is heard,
that roars through the universe.

April 2016
(written in February 2016)

Dear friend,

Are you really out there? Is there a movement out there at all? Is there any-one at all who is listening to me? Or am I deluding myself? Am I imagining something to protect myself from loneliness and indulge in an intoxicating sense of belonging?
We are talking about a movement that we are building together. But is there really such a thing? Don't worry, we are sober people. Not people who get carried away with things. We are not fooling ourselves. We know that there is no one out there. Running around out there are a lot of egomaniacs who want to have nothing to do with each other, all of whom are chasing the imaginations of their egos. Egomaniacs, who are not connected with each other in love. Isn't it so? We are alone. When we talk about movement, we mean the larger, impersonal movement of life, of love itself, that each one of us can join for himself, totally alone.

"Maybe we should once again talk about love," is what I recently proposed during a community evening. It had started to worry me, seeing attitudes arising in different corners of the fabric of our community, where some-thing is taken as love, which is obviously not.

Control, anxiety, possessiveness, becoming overly excited and enthusiastic, all these have nothing to do with love. On the contrary, they prevent it. To be in the state of love, is to be in a state in which not a trace of control exists and where fear has come completely to an end. And enthusiasm only raves about love and spreading love, in order to hide an underlying fear. Being in love is something quite different from this kind of overexcited elation. It is a silent happiness at having found someone to love, by whom one may perhaps even be loved in return.

All fear of not being loved or being abandoned has fallen away in the true state of being in love.

What do I mean by love? What is love really? How does one recognize love? Love is not really tangible. In a subsequent letter we will look at love more closely, but here and now we should concern ourselves once again with self-knowledge, with that which we have already been occupied in the last letter. For the moment, let the following suffice about love: It is like a calm lake, which spreads out within us or between us. It knows no unrest, no fear. One recognises it through its state of serenity, which gives us a sense of peace. Self-knowledge, accurate, honest self-knowledge, unerringly shows us whether we have encountered love within us, between us or in another.

Self-knowledge.

In the last newsletter we devoted ourselves to the tremendous importance of precise self-knowledge as a central tool of the movement that we form. Self-knowledge ultimately leads to the dissolution of the self in us, to its being overcome. If such is not the case, it means we are not serious enough, not precise enough, have not yet gone deep enough. Self-knowledge is the beginning of meditation. A turning inward to understand oneself, the world and relationships in all their contexts from the inside. Self-knowledge, through the overcoming of egocentricity, flows into what meditation really is in its depth. Self-knowledge leads to inner clarification, to the understanding of the self and its scheming ways. It brings order into our inner being, and thus also into our outer life, the tonal, to use an expression from the world of the Toltec warrior. Because, everything inside and outside is ultimately brought into order, the mind, the brain, can become completely still and therefore rise above the structures of the ego into the space of reality untouched by thought. Meditation opens in us the door to love and to the inexplicable.

To the *dreaming* and also to *dreaming* together that acts – as we have seen in it the second newsletter – as a potent force that can hold a movement together and give it direction. For anyone who finds access to this incredible thing everything else becomes secondary. Everything loses all meaning in the presence of this Absolute and Incomprehensible.

Like self-knowledge, meditation is a tool that serves to realize the concerns of our movement. Actually, both have no goal; aimless and ignorant we set out on this path, curious and eager to explore the reality, that which is. But in the end, we are met by that which alone is constant, that which determines and directs us from behind everything that is transitory. Without gaining access to the eternal and sacred, our lives remain stale and empty, superficial and meaningless. That which we delve into, as soon as self-knowledge and meditation open the door in the Inner, is indescribable, the Indescribable. Indeed it is nothing mysterious, nothing spectacular, nothing awesome related to visions, the supernatural or anything extrasensory. On the contrary, it is something quite "ordinary," but it is the Eternal, the Sacred, the only thing that matters. Meditation opens us for space, for the real, infinite space.

Self-knowledge, meditation, is the way to fathom out completely on your own, whether there is anything everlasting, anything eternal and sacred, anything absolute. Meditation, when practiced earnestly, ultimately leads to a life in this other space – which we, for example, describe as love – without running the danger of wanting to comprehend this love, this incomprehensible.

In the beginning, meditation is a penetration into the depths of the unfathomable, in order to clear out the last obstacles that keep closed the gateway to the very source of everything. Later, in the state of meditation, we occasionally dive into this source, breaking through to renew ourselves in it. But ultimately this space surrounds us completely, it becomes our home. We are allowed to live and act out of this state of meditation, of love. We become ready for a life beyond any control of will. From this point on, love itself takes over the leadership.

How does meditation work?

Meditation begins with self-knowledge. As soon as this comes to an end – in that the self, being completely permeated by consciousness, dissolves – the attention that has been freed up and sharpened by this process continues to explore the inner space of its own accord. Since everything in the realm of self has been put in order and understood through self-knowledge, the mind becomes calm. Thoughts fall silent and the brain is extraordinarily awake. It changes from being a thinking apparatus into a highly sensitive organ of perception, it discovers its broader function of deep perception, which was superimposed by the bare functionality of the machinery of memory and reproduction of the brain's computer, such that it was no longer accessible to our consciousness. The brain discovers its proper task as a highly sensitive instrument of perception that surrounds and directs the computer of knowledge and memory. The limited intelligence of intellectuality, so highly valued and overrated in the world today, submits itself to the much broader intelligence of a holistic view that gradually awakens in such a brain. The spirit, the free energy that we are, the awareness of the spark of consciousness that constitutes our being, becomes free to move within the space of the Inner, which at the same time is the real infinite space of the universe. It begins to explore that which lies beyond our thinking, which cannot be touched by it. What we call dreaming begins there. But also the insight into the nature of the Universal Spirit, the intention of love and of evolution. We become connected to an unlimited energy, the energy of love, and learn to surrender to it and let it direct our lives. We become its tool by allowing ourselves, time and again, to be flooded and renewed by this energy.

Self-knowledge teaches us to no longer avoid that which is, but rather to face it. Finally, our brain learns to give up any reaction to, any evasion of, that which is. In the end, the brain, the mind, becomes completely silent in this choiceless contemplation. A seeing becomes possible, a looking out of stillness, which can grasp reality directly. The halting of any emotional and mental response in the sense of defending against that which is, opens a gap to a completely different reality in which everything is determined by the energy of love. The persistent adherence to this process of self-knowledge widens this gap more and more, until one is finally swallowed up by the space which it opens. Whereas initially one dives only momentarily into this space of meditation, of love and stillness, ultimately one is admitted completely. Grace is imparted to you to be able to live entirely in this space.

"I reflected on everything that is accomplished by man on earth, and I concluded: Everything he has accomplished is futile - like chasing the wind," I often heard this verse in my childhood quoted from Ecclesiastes 1:14 in the Bible. A phrase that always appealed to me even when I was young. Today, the essence has caught up with me. The rain drops on the window pane mean more to me than the meeting of the Pope with the Orthodox patriarch after a thousand years. The rushing noise from outside, more than the questions on the ballot papers that want to be completed. Everything has no meaning in the face of the Great and the Sacred that light up in the very small and the profane. In the face of love, the unfathomable mystery of our being. Not that I would in anyway feel less than joyful, if scientists can prove the existence of gravitational waves using irresponsibly great resources a hundred years after they were calculated by Einstein, even though I actually think, we should first take care of the hunger on earth and only then tackle the soaring heights of what is knowable. But then both seem so completely meaningless to me in the face of the knowledge of the finiteness of everything and the perspective of only the Absolute, which my heart can sense.

Are you out there, dear friend? Are you tuned in to the great movement of life, of love? Do you stand completely alone and therefore belong to it? Or do you not exist at all as a part of this movement?

May happiness be with you

Samuel Widmer Nicolet

PS: In the meantime, the criminal investigation that has been initiated against us still awaits the decision of the Federal Supreme Court regarding the unsealing of files that have been seized and which are subject to medical confidentiality.

As yet, the allegations are still insufficient for an indictment. In any case, after more than a year, the matter continues to languish without direction. In the appendix, I enclose my second letter to the prosecutor, which I sent to him in September 2015 after six months of waiting, and with which I kept trying to bring relationship into the picture.

Attachment: 2. Letter to the prosecutor of 10th September 2015 including supplements

[The referred to supplementary material were provided to the public prosecutor but could not for tactical reasons be published as part of the 4th Newsletter.]

A wedding poem

Absolutely and whole heartedly I love you
Despite all my inner unrest, chimes in me
the most ardent love song for you

When life afflicts you, making you fragile and tender,
this activates all protective instincts in me
So great is the love for you in me

I search for something earnest and beautiful,
for a wedding poem to make you happy
My sweetheart, oh apple of my eye, my millennium love

Thus, I think of you, of us
All world's stress scarcely attunes me to poetry,
finds me more disposed to stupid, tactless jokes

What a joy to hear from you
even if sometimes I hardly know anymore
whether I can believe yet longer in love

Maybe a creative impulse overcomes me
when I let my thoughts rest with you
poised to sing your love song

September 10, 2015

Department of Public Prosecution
For the attention of Mr Claudio Ravicini
Franziskanerhof
Barfüssergasse 28
P.O. Box 157

4502 Solothurn

Further personal questions

Dear Mr Ravicini

During our first and only real conversation, you asked at the door, how many children I still had to take care of. I answered "seven," but in fact there are eight. I liked the fact that you also have an eye for that which is essential.

It has now been almost half a year since this memorable day and I thought I could write to you once again. This time around, as a precaution, I asked "Mama" Kury if I could directly get in touch with "Papa" Ravicini. She allowed it.

Isn't it a bit crazy how much I have been preoccupied with you in the past few months and you obviously with me too without us ever having talked again? From what you write about me in different contexts, I realize that you are trying to understand what is really going on with us. In doing this it strikes me that you do not as yet perceive everything in terms of reality. So, I thought, I could send you at least part of a small text I composed for our lawyers about myself, my work, and what moves me. Maybe it will help to put things in the right perspective. Meanwhile, additionally, we had this unfortunate incident and even a small clash. At the moment however, I do not want to comment on it. I have to first somewhat digest it.

Just imagine, you could prove to me, what you want to prove to me (and as is well known that what the truth is in such a game is yet another question)! What would happen then?

Would you take the responsibility for my children out of my hands? So as to care for them better and to do better with them? For my women? The community of partially mentally impaired people for whom I am responsible?

What would be better then? What is it all about? What is actually essential? And what would be proven? That a cow eats what it wants, or that it has no horns, because the farmer wants it that way?

So be it! It's all fine with me. What can happen to someone, once you have basically accepted their fate? Already for some time above the retirement age, it would perhaps even be a relief for me to be in whatever way discharged from duty. And what would you get from it? Except maybe a dark satisfaction? That is to say, you are keeping me on my toes with your investigation. If this continues, I'll have to quit my job to keep pace with your tempo regarding injunctions, submissions, and new, hasty actions. As a pensioner, this might anyway be sensible.

Only, who will then care for my children? Is the idea that I should get in touch with the welfare department as a precaution? Especially since you (or someone?) really seem (seems) anxious to at least destroy our business if you cannot get us any other way.

What I would like to know from you in this regard: Is there actually a right of appeal against indefensible excessive demands in connection with a criminal investigation?

Yes, what is essential? And what is it really all about?

We have already spoken briefly about fate in our first conversation. I have just completed a book on dying and death, in which much is said about acknowledging one's destiny and the serenity that comes from it. I will send you a copy with this letter. The book is explicitly not intended as a gift, but as further evidence of what I do and what I am actually engaged with. I am not concerned with bribing you or anything like that, but with supporting you in your endeavour to look behind the scenes of my work which I feel I recognise in you.

Do you know what honestly surprised me when reading your submissions and all the written and sometimes almost overwhelming communication? That you're not assuming innocence, but rather proven guilt. In the meantime, I think that as a prosecutor this is probably your job, about which I wrote the last time, and that I am convinced that you conscientiously fulfil this role. I am really new to this business and learn new things about it every day. Yet, your behaviour has left me uncertain as to whether you really care about what is essential. Also when I read the reasoning and evidence of the Superior Court regarding the matter of seizure, which in essence succinctly states that the accused must be guilty if he is accused, I am wondering if, after thirty years of being bullied in canton Solothurn, a fair judicial process can be at all expected. Fortunately, there is still a federal court.

As I said, I will send you all this to help prepare for our next real conversation, which I hope will take place someday. From my point of view, the information about the context in our case should help to facilitate the discussion and to clarify it in advance, so there is no need for unnecessary misunderstandings and delays. As you can see from the documents, there are other parts of my text, which I will provide you with at a later date, depending on how the issues evolve. For part of it, that which concerns the slanderers, Sabine Bundschu and Ariela Bogenberger, as well as the two Beckmann fraudsters, it would be necessary, however, for you to obtain or order a release from medical confidentiality for me, so that I can provide you with some incriminating documents (part 3 and part 9). I would be grateful for this.

In a second appendix you will also find additional statements regarding the unsealing process that I have provided our lawyers in order to facilitate their work. Within, you may also find some puzzle pieces, which can give you a clearer picture of us.

May your wishes come true.

With best regards

Dr. med. P. Samuel Widmer Nicolet

Enclosures:
- Statement regarding the allegations concerning offenses against the narcotics act (incomplete version)
- Statement regarding the application for unsealing
- The unsealing process
- Comments regarding the statement of the public prosecutor in the unsealing process

[The supplementary material provided to Mr Ravicini, could not for tactical reasons be included as attachments to 4th Newsletter.]

Priority list?

1. To love
All around and with nothing but nothing in return.

2. We
To arrange oneself with everything and organise one's entire life
in such a way, so that all of us are doing well and so that we are
consistently happy and in the right state.

3. You
The same from me most of all for you.

4. Sexuality
To arrange oneself with everything and organise everything
surrounding one's entire life in such a way, so that sexuality remains
joyful and there is at all times enough energy available to be
orgastically potent and disposed to love.

5. The same as under 2 and 3, applied to further relationships and
love stories.

6. Responsibility and obligations in the family, the community, in
work and in one's vocation, in the world and the community of all
beings.

7. The nonessential
Such as becoming angry and agitated, reading cartoon comics,
engrossing oneself in nonessential relationships, etc. etc....

May 2016

Dear friends

The fact that we form a movement together does not mean that we belong to a group, that we submit to some authority. It simply means that we pursue common concerns, common interests, concern ourselves with meaningful things together, work cooperatively in the same field. Each individual stands alone in such a movement, he is a light unto himself. He is free. This is easily recognized by the fact that such movements hardly have any organizational structures. We are not an organization, we form a living being in motion.

Before we turn in the coming newsletters to the special tools that support us in self-knowledge, we first want to deal with love as we announced in the last newsletter. It is our interest in these tools – in Tantra, psycholysis and community-making – that unites us externally in the movement we form. But inwardly it is the love for which these tools ultimately stand, the strength of their flow between us that is responsible for the cohesion among us or its absence. We do not just want to deal with the tools in the coming contributions, we also want to explore the "goals" that they strive for, the deep dimensions of consciousness that psycholysis wants to bring to light, the tantric visions given birth by the tantric process, the true community that we struggle for in the process of community making. But also the individual steps – the most important components of the self-knowledge process that forms the connecting element between all these insights – will occupy us for a long time in further letters.

Yet behind and above all of this stands love, this wonderful being. In everything that interests us, it is she who determines what happens and who alone is essential. All self-knowledge leads to her, all deep exploration, all tantric visions, all true community is about her. All tools point to her, all struggle in the individual stages of self-knowledge and ultimately in this process of going beyond the self, tell only of her. She is the light within that we are looking for, one's own light, that everyone has to find themselves and orientate themselves by, that ultimately radiates far beyond everything that is one's own.

That is why we want to turn to her, to love, before we lose ourselves in the details of the work of self-knowledge. She, who is the real goal in everything, the real link, the secret and the everlasting behind all striving.

How quickly everything that was meant to be love can turn into something ugly! Is it not amazing to observe this? Is love not abandoned in the end by most people who then prefer to stand on the side of those who condemn it and persecute it out of cowardice? But how can you betray her once you have realized in the process of self-knowledge that you yourself are love.

The feeling of the Whole is love, is happiness. Does everyone, as much as they may hunger for love, only get a share of it to the extent that they can hold the Whole within them? Often one feels left alone with love and not carried with it. It seems to be love's fate to have to stand alone with the unique, the wonderful, the special that it contains. Will we human beings ever find, discover or create a place where love and trust are a matter of course and where fear and control are silent, held by an alert mind? To expect something other than the normal, other than fear and control, is the presumptuousness to which love surrenders itself again and again. It has the courage to be left all alone.

Love does not belong to us. if love in us is not complete, if it is not allowed to fill us completely, if we do not allow it, if we prevent it through control and fear, if everything, every feeling, has not perfectly found its place in us, it makes it impossible for us to see love completely, to let her take us completely and lead us. Love holds and embraces everything that non-love cannot hold within itself. This separates non-love from love, and she cannot bridge the gap that is created by it, even though she encompasses everything, even this separation, even though she is the One.

How do you find out what is right in a situation, what is harmonious, what needs to be done? Can someone tell you? No one can tell you. You have to find out for yourself, discover by honest self-knowledge what the right thing is, and afterwards you have to take responsibility for it yourself. That makes you self-reliant, autonomous, independent. That makes you free.
There is no control in love. That is why, even among people, there must be no control over each other. Everyone must find from out of themselves their way, the truth, the right thing and the harmonious thing. From the flowing together of what results from each individual, arises true community, a true movement that can bring about true change.
Love follows the awareness, which is switched off through control. Fully developed awareness is love. Love flows in it. The right and harmonious unfolds between us, and in our lives, when awareness is there, when energy follows this choiceless awareness, when awareness has the lead and extinguishes in us every fear and tendency to control

Love is the light within that we finally liberate within ourselves through the process of self-knowledge. This love is the law. It is the only law that the lover follows. This makes him or her autonomous, independent, able to stand alone. And yet this love is nothing personal. It does not belong to us. In each one of us, it is the same love that we finally discover as our true "self" within ourselves. In it we are one. In it, if we are awakened for it, we are united and welded into a movement and into a true, conflict-free community. In it we agree on everything, see the same reality and truth, without being compliant, without conforming to anything. This love, to which we finally gain access within, guides us. Her voice within us is our conscience. She unerringly shows us what is good, what is right. She gifts us her morality, the morality of love, in which there is no oppression, but a natural virtuousness blossoms.
Paradoxically, we find our true individuality, our very own authentic pure being that wants to express itself in its very own way in surrendering to the unity of all, which this entity "Love" embodies, to which we can open a door in our innermost being. This "own" blossoms out of the completely imper-

sonal of love without any egocentricity. Love is a being, independent from us, that fills the whole universe. We can open ourselves to it or refuse it. In relation to each other, this love manifests itself in our ability to really listen to each other, to connect deeply with each other, in the compassion we feel for each other, in the ability to make ourselves available with the same passion and same intensity for a common intention and to work together and to cooperate therein without conflict. It gives us a communion of heart that can create and find a connection beyond words.

Love in us, if we release it and let it work in us without any control, opens the door to the depth of being, to the holy and everlasting, to that for which there are no words. To the Great. To the timeless Eternal. To the Other.

If we allow the love within us to show us what is good, what is right, if many people allow it, a movement of good, a new story, a good society will come into being all by itself. Ultimately, this is the main goal of the movement we form. A goal that cannot be organized, a goal that wants to blossom by itself from the self-knowledge of the individual. A good, healthy society must be the main goal. It cannot be organized. Rather, the question is whether we humans learn to allow the self-organizing power and intelligence of love to take the lead and produce a healthy world. Care, diligence, responsibility, these qualities of love come by themselves from the awareness that the lover has found, from the stillness into which his path of self-enquiry has led him. Only from stillness is real relationship possible, loving relationship. From out of a still looking arises direct encounter with others, which neither contains nor has to overcome any distance, no images about each other, no separating thoughts. Only in such relatedness does the energy of love flow freely. Love is real relationship. Real relationship is love. The free being of love flows into us and begins to work creatively through us as soon as we have created the conditions for it in ourselves through self-knowledge. The prerequisites are stillness of the mind, an inner emptiness, the overcoming of all egocentricity. To be devoted to love paradoxically means to have found ones true "self". To insist on an ego, on the other hand, is to be alienated from oneself. Paradoxes!

The most important and fundamental concerns of the movement we form, the concerns we wish to examine, are all based on the presence of love. Without love, all spiritual searching and psychological exploration, all meditation and striving for knowledge have no basis, no deep meaning, no sense. That is why we put love first. It is, to a degree, the "result" that we strive for in the process of self-knowledge. But without it accompanying and leading this process from the beginning, it will not lead anywhere. Love is the compassionate intelligence out of which all our actions must flow, therefore we invite love to us in advance of all insight that in the end comes out of her.

"Did we not come to make the earth a paradise?" I previously asked in my first newsletter. Isn't this our real goal? Aren't we part of the movement that intends something like this, dreams of something like this?
We do not really form a movement. That would be something organized, something of thoughts, created and produced by the ego. We are part of the movement, which is led by love. For this fundamental movement in the universe we are awakened. The goal of this force, if it can be called a goal at all, is renewal. The renewal of us humans and therefore of our world. It is love that renews everything over and over again.
Are we awakened for this?

May love be with you

Samuel Widmer Nicolet

PS: Also this time, a few lines of orientation for those who would like to be informed about the further course of the investigation that was initiated against us as a result of a legal complaint. We are still waiting for the decision of the Federal Supreme Court, which should determine the preconditions for any possible later prosecution.
Also this time, I have attached one of my letters, which I have sent every three months to the leading public prosecutor. It is the third of these letters dated 14th December 2015. And also the answer I received.

[Here also, we have for tactical reasons abstained from including as attachments to the 5th newsletter those attachments that were also withheld from the public prosecutor.]

Freedom

The wind sweeps gently through dark treetops,
The day is mild, the sky wide.
To strive for the highest peak,
The people below lack time.

Yet even up there almost by the Great,
Tranquillity never remains untouched.
The people perform their antics,
The eagle circles, as is his due.

Mankind, do you want to find stillness,
Raise yourself up like the eagle!
Constraint must never bind you,
And fate? – Expand, oh fate!

14th December 2015

Department of Public Prosecution
For the attention of Mr Claudio Ravicini
Franziskanerhof
Barfüssergasse 28
P.O. Box 157

4502 Solothurn

More personal questions

Dear Mr Ravicini

Do you also sometimes look out of the window at a late hour to see the moon and the stars on a clear night?
Sometimes I wonder if I would have become a better cellist if I had serenaded the moon.

Once again another three months have passed and actually we have not made any progress. Of course, I too am thinking about how we could find a solution in this muddled and burdensome story.
Shortly before my second personal letter to you, with the help of the police and your colleagues, you once again intruded on us, and I wrote to you afterwards that I did not want to comment on this yet. I wanted to first digest this hurtful story, which was also degenerating into aggression.
"I don't have to listen to that," you exclaimed before you left the room upset. Aren't you really obliged to listen when there's something to criticize? A rather high-handed attitude, of which strangely I am often accused: that I would not tolerate criticism? You even threatened to imprison me when you became angry because I didn't agree with everything you ordered. Yes, of course, that's how it is! You are the power! Even if you are not in the right.

Once again another three months have passed and actually we have not made any progress. Of course, I too am thinking about how we could find a solution in this muddled and burdensome story.

You see, if you proceed according to your usual pattern and seek to penetrate us and look into everything by means of force, by means of state power, you are forcing me and us to defend and barricade ourselves. You cannot look uninvited into the secrets of our patients. We must defend ourselves and their rights. We have no other choice.

On the other hand, it is not our way to deny someone an insight into our lives and activities. Actually, we are very open-minded people and everyone is allowed to look in on us unhindered. Just like the journalists from Beckmann- or the Blick. We are not used to deviating from this attitude, and it causes a very peculiar mood in our everyday life.

It would therefore be conceivable for us to invite you, and as far as I am concerned together with the cantonal physician, and give you the opportunity to participate in everything we do, or rather to apply to participate, just as our patients do or the Beckmann fraudsters have done.

Could you imagine, for example, being involved in everything we do for a year? You, or someone you designate, would accompany us in everything we do and become part of it. Would this not be a way of settling this absurd dispute? It could also help to rein in the unbelievable defamations that have been increasingly ballooning into an organised pogrom in the media for years. What do you think: would this not be a sensible investigative strategy?

I also wanted to inform you that I have decided to make public on the Internet everything that is going on between us. That is including my personal letters to you. Not immediately, but when it seems important to me in future processes. It is becoming increasingly clear to me that our issue is not just about me, but also about a fundamental dispute for which I would like to motivate the public. Well, you (and your backers) have already been doing this the whole time.

We actually wanted to send you in the supplement a more complete version of the statement that you have already received with my last letter. I thought that it's about time to let the cat out of the bag about what we're really doing. You would have therefore received again everything I wrote down about it, but this time supplemented by parts 5 and 8, which should be particularly informative for you.

Naive as I am, I hoped they would give you a fairly complete picture of our reality. Point 5 is the actual counterstatement to the slander of the two ladies, Bundschu and Bogenberger. The fact that I only wanted to present these now has to do, on the one hand, with the fact that you never asked me about it, but on the other hand, also with the fact that I am reluctant to disclose the facts which are presented in it. Not because it would be about something illegal, but because something worth protecting might lose its protection. However, parts 3 and 9 would still have remained outstanding after this. I will not comment on these until it is necessary in any legal proceedings and I am allowed to do so with regard to medical secrecy. Regarding this final clarification, you would have anyway still needed to be patient. In addition, just like last time, you would have also received a small number of recent communications to our lawyers, which might have also been informative for you.

But this time "Mama" Kury does not agree. She thinks I would be playing into your hands if I just simply disclosed "our/her strategy".

I am not cut out for this. I think everything would be a lot easier and less complicated if we just put all our cards on the table. But I'm learning. We play games. Maybe it's not about truth at all. That's why I cannot (yet) give you the supplements mentioned. Unless you convince me that I should do it after all (which I would like best).

You reacted briefly but friendly to my first letter. In regards to the second you said nothing further. It doesn't really feel friendly anymore. Nevertheless, I dare to write to you again. If you are not interested in a real relationship, please tell me. I am well aware that it may be totally unwise to harass you in this way. But perhaps you have already realised that I am less concerned with being wise and thus averting or minimising any condemnation. If there is still an opportunity, I will probably tell you something about my actual motives next time.

Unfortunately, my positive impression of the first encounter with you has evaporated due to the contacts that have since then been rather devoid of relationship and this has made room for all sorts of question marks. For example, I wonder how it is that you seem to have a personal interest in this matter, which leads you to be carried away into more emotions than I, the one who is ultimately severely affected. Not only as a psychiatrist and psychotherapist, but also as a human being, I am accustomed to striving for clarification of issues, of whatever kind they may be, through genuine relationship discussion. I'm surprised that people in your profession don't seem to place much value on it. In my experience, in this way, everything eventually comes to light and can be understood.

Buddha allegedly defined truth in the following way: "Truth is what works". A good title, I think, for our discussion.

Since my last letter I have suffered a heart attack. The second after almost 18 years. It makes sense to me that my heart wants to break during this present time.

The moon shines brightly into the nocturnal bedchamber and through its cosmic aura it reminds us of the mystery, to which we are all ultimately more committed than to all fleeting, earthly games.

I wish you a merry Christmas and send friendly greetings

Samuel Widmer Nicolet

Unfortunately not enclosed:
- Our statement supplemented by parts 5 and 8
- Mail to Mrs Kury etc. of 21st September 2015 regarding:
  - Clarifications of medical secrecy/ professional secrecy/ protection of privacy
  - Supplementary comments from a legally knowledgeable colleague
- Mail of 21st September 2015 to Mrs Kury regarding the request to unseal the recording device

[Also for the 5th newsletter, we have for tactical reasons not included the supplementary material]

A new light

Defiant peaks, wrapped in swaths,
Billowing fog, undulating far and wide,
Cloudy light, clenching to oneness,
Let us bathe in holy fire.

Farewell is at hand and new laughter.
Let doubt and eternal question be!
Criticism is not valid, unless it dares,
To be obligated to do better.

Sun breaks through and brings life back,
Warmth invites you to be carefree.
But the scent of autumn reminds us finely
Of dying, death and their silent striving.

Public Prosecutor

*Franziskanerhof
Barfüssergasse 28, Postfach 157
4502 Solothurn
Telefon 032 627 60 40
Telefax 032 627 60 41*

Mr
Paul Samuel Widmer Nicolet
Rebe 138
4574 Nennigkofen

22 December 2015

Dear Dr. Widmer

I have received your letter "Even more personal questions" of 14 December 2015. However, only after the holidays will I be able to give you a substantiated answer - provided this seems at all appropriate due to the different procedural roles already mentioned.

I kindly ask you to please take note and wish you an enjoyable holiday and a pleasant time.

Yours sincerely
The prosecutor

C. Ravicini

Goes to
Paul Samuel Widmer Nicolet, Rebe 138, 4574 Nennigkofen, by priority mail

it is almost morning
a waning moon falls in love
with a brightest morning star
on heavy wings
a night bird floats
between the two
into the unattainable

solemn flaps of wings

far in the east a first glow
the chance of the eternally new
lies innocently above all
the freshness of the new day
caresses the displeasure of the night
life seems to be tender
I think of you

Newsletter 6:
Community-Making

June 2016
(written in mid-April)

Dearest friends,

Our life, our whole being, all existence is like a dream, transitory like a dream. Everything that appears will pass away again. We know vaguely how to distinguish a fleeting dream of the night from the material experience of our day's hard reality. But when we try to grasp this difference, we quickly doubt whether there is an essential difference at all. Everything is ephemeral, all striving is just chasing the wind. Nothing remains at the end. We and everything, whatever counts together with us as existing, belong to the transitory. Everything is only a dream, only an ephemeral dream.

Is it therefore surprising that people have always searched for something that is everlasting, that is eternal? Is there something that is not subject to time, that can escape the dictate of death? Something that does not know death? Is there something in us that corresponds to this?

In the last newsletter we extolled love. Is it her, the only one who remains at the end? After all, is what remains of us merely what we have added to her, to the sea of love? Is she the timeless Holy behind all apparitions that are born of her and endlessly die again into her, the ultimate reality and truth in the depths of all being?

In the process of self-knowledge, to which we have dedicated ourselves out of insight into its necessity, we face up to that which is. We try to fathom what is in us, in our relationships, in our life situations. That which is, may not yet be the truth. It is what is. It is our reality, the reality of appearances. To understand, to fathom, to see that which is, however, forms the basis to finally go beyond it, to finally recognize the truths behind appearances, to take root in what is deeper. Finally, in the one reality, the ultimate truth of the unity of everything, of the love that underlies everything. The only thing that is eternal, that which is not transient, that which is true.

That which is, is our ego and everything that arises and has arisen from its thinking. The truth is the love behind this dream, the One, and everything that comes out from her and into manifestation.

In this letter we will begin by describing the special tools that help us to support ourselves in the process of self-knowledge. Tantra, psycholysis, community-making. We have claimed that these aids are what unite us externally in the movement that we form and that expressed in these aids is the love for which they ultimately stand and thus the cohesion of our movement that depends on their flow.

Let us begin today with community-making[6]. Community making, of course, aims at something, at authentic and ultimately true community, that is, at the manifestation of love, at the materialization of the inner eternal at the level of the outer transient appearance. But we will talk about this in a later letter. First of all, community building is primarily a helpful instrument for self-exploration. In sharing, i.e. in the mutual exchange within a group process, in sharing one's thoughts and feelings, one comes closer to each other, one faces each other's truth and the truth between one another, and one goes beyond superficial encounter into a process of really getting involved with one another.

Ultimately, community building naturally has the goal of bringing about real community. But initially it is a goal in itself. In the confrontation with others and above all with oneself that it stimulates, one begins to encoun-

---

[6] I talk more extensively about community-making in my book about community:
Samuel Widmer Nicolet: Living Together, Community and Community-Making; BasicIndia Editions, 2017

ter the reality of what actually is. One stops deluding oneself. Almost by itself all one's illusions fall away, one sheds all erroneous conceptions, one overcomes being deadlocked in opinions and hardened points of view. The conditioning to which one has been and is subjected becomes visible. How it fosters entanglement in different conditioning becomes apparent. In becoming still together, showing oneself vulnerable and emptying oneself of all assumptions and fixed points of view, one enters into the feeling of community, into the fundamental that unites us all.

There is nothing that more easily helps us to correct our obsession with absurdities and self-will and open ourselves to the inevitability of finding consensus than to surrender ourselves to a continuous and committed group process. The insight into the fact that we humans are all the same in a certain sense and that we all have the same needs and all need the same consideration – so necessary as a prerequisite for the emergence of love – ultimately prevails quite easily in self-experience groups and even more so in a community where everyone is involved with each other. The awakening for love, for her to be the solution for everything and the only solution at all for the human problem, comes from this.

It is earnestness and honesty that relieves the group meeting of the superficiality and noncommittal nature of pseudo-community banality. These are absolutely necessary. A certain passion for genuineness and authenticity. Without the willingness to face unpleasant truths and confrontations, even extensive sitting together will not create a deep connection. This also includes walking together through chaotic phases and times of disappointment and hopelessness without running away. A certain perseverance, an intention to stick to it, helps. And these, of course, come from love for each other, which paradoxically is both a prerequisite and a goal for all togetherness. Without being mutually close to each other's hearts, there will be no community between us human beings. It is undisputed that this warmth of heart for each other is awakened and nurtured in the community-making process. But without already having access to it, we will hardly get involved in it. It needs the open ear, the open heart.

The main topics in community-making are mainly conflict resolution (chaos), healing (emptying) and being able to understand each other (community feeling). But almost unnoticed in the background, what happens most of all is self-knowledge, which is an indispensable prerequisite for it. Seeing oneself as one really is, initiates a transformation through which one renews, purifies and recreates oneself. Often the process of community building seems laborious, fruitless and endless with no result in terms of the emergence of common thinking and acting. For the individual within, this process can nevertheless become a resounding success, as long as he uses it to get to know himself better in the mirror of relationships. To have finally understood oneself through and through will show him the possibility of freeing himself from the dominion of the self to which he is subjected, and thus of becoming a bearer of the community feeling, of love.

Outside, spring is breaking through. Despite the changeable weather, the cherry trees literally explode in their flowering splendour. The magnolias, the pear trees and many others are also following on. Bright green already begins to show itself everywhere.

Everything becomes new again. After a long hibernation, after half a year of nature's dying and retreat, nature breaks out again as if for the very first time. Tabula rasa. And then again a new beginning. Nature, that which is alive, understands this principle.

This is what mankind lacks, what it has lost. The ability to wipe everything off the table and to start anew. We humans have forgotten how to orient ourselves by life.

Self-knowledge brings us back the connection to the natural. It makes us empty, empties us of all patterns of conditioning and of all past guilt that have accumulated in us over time. We regain the possibility to continuously check our inner inventory, to sort out what has become obsolete and unusable, and to look at everything completely anew. It makes the ending of all neurosis conceivable.

To be able to start over again, what mercy! To be able to start anew from time to time, a very important part of the self-knowledge process. This would be so needed for the whole of humanity. It would be so easy to regain the skill. In the sharing of the community-making process it takes place, we find it again, it finally comes to the emptying of everything old, we are completely renewed from within in the emergence of the community feeling.

Love must be able to renew itself, otherwise it degenerates. Relationships must be able to renew themselves, otherwise dust settles on them and they ossify into customs and habits. Everything must be allowed from time to time to be questioned, to be reconsidered, to start anew. Freedom from taboos.

Community-making is the first, and an outstanding tool for self-knowledge, and at the same time the emergence of community is also the result and expression of thorough, earnest and honest self-exploration. If community does not in the end blossom from it, self-knowledge is worth nothing, is without meaning, is not exact and truthful.
The other two tools, psycholysis and Tantra, to which our movement is dedicated and which we will cover in the coming months, assist self-knowledge by supporting community making. The goals of community-making – true community – of psycholysis – awakening into the deep dimensions of our being – and Tantra – the tantric visions – reveal themselves as we move forward. The many facets and subtleties of true self-knowledge are illuminated in this process from all sides and thus understood. The self overcomes itself through insight into itself and liberates itself into the Great. To be a free energy.

Outside spring is calling. Already in the early hours of the morning we are enchanted by the manifold birdcalls with their uplifting tapestry of sound. When the sun breaks through the clouds, it quickly becomes warm, and the glittery drops on the fresh flowers and new leaves quickly disappear. A jubilation is in the air and the heart bounds towards it. The heaviness of the dark days of winter is forgotten. Everything is new. And everything is a dream.
Awaken from the dream!

May awakening come to you

Samuel Widmer Nicolet

PS: Regarding the criminal investigation in which we were involved, there is the following news to report for those who are interested:

In the meantime, the Federal Supreme Court has finally decided to what extent seized files may or may not be inspected.

Also attached to this newsletter is my fourth personal letter to the chief public prosecutor dated 13 March 2016, one year after the start of the criminal investigation.

Oh love, not only of one life,
but a whole eternity!
What a beautiful morning today!
Full of light. So still.
Oh, what golden freedom shows itself,
once for an hour no one is there.

No matter how much one loves people,
however much, if one has luck,
they might spoil one,
they are always a burden,
with their narrowness and absent
oneness with the vastness.

Only rarely do you meet someone,
in whose presence the heavens
remain great, the earth beauty,
the eternity without end.
Like you.
What a blessing!

To my good fortune
an occasional hour suffices.
You too seem to lie awake
this night?
Yet it was not worries that drove me
from my bed, but happiness.

Happiness,
to already feel the recovery again.
Truly, after my heart they have now
also broken my spine.
I am barely able
to kindle even a small fire.

For this the inner fire is blazing
all the higher, and burns
to write you poems.
The love of a whole life,
of a whole eternity,
I am to you.

13 March 2016

Department of Public Prosecution
For the attention of Mr Claudio Ravicini
Franziskanerhof
Barfüssergasse 28
P.O. Box 157

4502 Solothurn

And yet more personal questions

Dear Mr Ravicini

Soon it will be a year since we met. Soon my wife is celebrating her birthday again. This time marking a decade. On March 19, a date that has now gained a completely different meaning as anniversary.
Have you seen the new Heidi film? Did you also cry alongside your children about a lost world? I met there the Chief Judge and Vice President of the Higher Court, Daniel Kiefer, whom I have known personally since my professional beginnings in Solothurn – he himself, like me, at the very beginning of a career. In the brief exchange that we had, did he also think about the fact that we might soon have something to do with each other? Or do friendly feelings leave you biased? Does one have to be angry with each other to find the truth and speak justice?

In your short friendly reply to my first personal letter, you wrote that I would understand that you, as the leader of the investigation against me, would not be allowed to talk to me. In the somewhat longer, more polite than friendly answer to my last, third letter of December 14, you reaffirmed this. Honestly, I must confess to you: "No, I don't understand that." On the contrary, I think you should talk to me above all else. That is why I continue to write to you in order to compensate a little for the lack I feel in this regard.

In my last letter, I promised to tell you something about my motives in our proceedings. I mentioned earlier that this could be unwise and that my lawyer will certainly find it unwise. I also mentioned that this is meaningless for me, because I am interested in something other than by any means going unpunished.

I don't know whether you have realised in the meantime what it is that I am really interested in.

I want to bring about something, bring it about completely as a whole. Of course, I also want to prove my innocence. But primarily this is not important. If necessary, I accept that I also have to become a martyr of our cause. It's about something completely different. It's not just about psycholysis either. Psycholysis is more an external symbol for it. I called it a better world already in my first letter to you. I want to bring about a better world. For this I give everything. For this I have given my life. For this I am also ready to die. Isn't it strange that it arouses suspicion when you stand up for something? Suspicion of being a sect.

In fact, we see ourselves as an oppressed political minority who want to save the endangered, millennia-old legacy of shamanism (a medical means of healing) from extermination and protect the associated fundamental human rights from unlawful and ignorant prohibitions. And also this stands only symbolically for something still much more comprehensive, which I do not at all want to define further. A better world may suffice as an expression of it.

Unfortunately, your detailed answer to my last letter, which you announced in your short letter of December 22, never reached me. I don't know what you possibly might have had to tell me. As far as I am concerned, I have further questions:

Don't you think it's time to finally close the matter? Actually, we were harassed enough, weren't we? Put under stress and defamed in public. Our lives intrusively invaded. You plundered our cash boxes. I know, I know, that was just your job. Don't you think it's enough? And for what? What are you accusing us of?

The existence of families is being destroyed unscrupulously - and why? We didn't harm anyone, we didn't kill anyone. We merely defend human values and do good all round. I suppose you know of Raif Badawi, the Saudi Arabian blogger who has been in prison for ten years and is waiting for the remaining nine hundred and fifty lashes ordered to him. The entire Western world is outraged that a person is treated this way simply because he expresses his opinion. But is it really different here? Certainly, the methods of punishment in this country are no longer so drastic, no longer physical. But rather psychological. Because if you seriously give attention to the media smear campaign[7] of the last thirty years, which was led against me and us, and if you seriously compare its agitation with the facts of our lives, you will have to admit that there is no freedom of opinion here either. And when I see how you, too, allow yourself to be influenced by it in your statements about our investigation and again and again let yourself be carried away by it in your submissions to the point of creating propaganda instead of committing yourself to finding the truth, it does make one wonder.

As a result of these vilifications, our practice has been inspected and audited several times and in various respects over the years, including specifically regarding the use of narcotics, by the cantonal pharmacist, by the cantonal physician and once even by the BAG (Bundesamt für Gesundheit) [FOPH Federal Office of Public Health]. Marco Schärer said years ago that we were the best audited medical practice in the canton. Not a single irregularity was detected. The FOPH's inspection even took place unannounced during a seminar. These official results obviously contradict the allegations of Bundschu/ Bogenberger and a sensationalistic journalism. Do you ever think about it? Freedom of the press apparently means that journalists are allowed to put out any nonsense that goes through their minds. Or do you really think I would abuse children and rape patients? However, the scribblers, who are only allowed to say what their politically controlled bosses tell them

---

[7] Recently reviewed in the bachelor thesis of a student, if you are interested (Rahel Nicolet: Die mediale Darstellung der Psycholyse/ Eine Untersuchung über die letzten zwei Jahrzehnte am Beispiel ausgewählter Schweizer Printmedien; Universität Freiburg (CH); 2016) [The media presentation of psycholysis/ A study of the last two decades using selected Swiss print media as examples; University of Fribourg (CH); 2016)]

to do, must have a good nose for who has been declared outlawed by the society in question, otherwise they will soon be in trouble themselves.

Do you think it's acceptable to put in such an effort, to waste so much taxpayers' money just to destroy someone? And for what? Would it not be wiser to turn to the real problems of which there are truly enough in the world? Legality seems to me to be an elastic concept. If one only considers that all the crimes committed by the state in the course of history – such as the crimes of National Socialism or all the other genocides and ethnic cleansings – were absolutely legal in their time and place, or that we know of countless dissidents whose behaviour was and is branded illegal by the same state authorities even though we all know that they were and are more than innocent. Or think of the state's dealings here in Switzerland with Romani people and "Verdingkinder" [indentured child labourers], for which we must apologise today. Are you sure that there will not be at some point, when we are no longer there and have nothing to gain from it, also a rehabilitation procedure concerning the "Kirschblütler" [people associated with the Kirschbluete community], which will call into question the use of your henchmen in official injustice? For even if at the time of the event everyone questioning institutional authority is punished and bullied, years later and with regard to the past, the same authority gladly and unrestrainedly demands that everyone should have stood courageously like a William Tell if he thought he discovered illegality in the actions of the state authority.

What can you, what can anyone really accuse me of? At every point you try to come up with something that I and we might have done wrong. But I didn't do anything wrong. I have done an excellent job all my life for which there would be every reason to be grateful to me and to appreciate me. And should I ever actually be punished, it will be precisely because I did not bow my head to Gessler's hat.
But if we were acquitted (which is also in the realm of possibilities of an unpredictable justice), will someone pay us for the damage that has been done, the many hours we have spent on this stupidity, the worries we have had to endure?
Don't you think it's about enough, that it suffices and that you and everyone else can finally leave us alone again? If we had more personal contact

with each other, I would ask you if you are not fed up giving your life for something like this, for something that is ultimately completely insignificant. Yes, it's just your job, you assured me. But how can you be happy in such a job? But I already asked you in my first letter if you would like to join me and take a stand for a better world.

I know you will probably say: Let's wait and see what the Federal Supreme Court decides in the matter of unsealing. But I can assure you that you won't find anything that incriminates us there either. Even if the court should decide along the same line as the court of lower instance, you will be left empty-handed. We are fighting for nothing using a lot of effort and a lot of money. Fortunately, the plundered cash boxes are once again in good health. On a further visit you would find them in the very same place.

If you haven't seen the new Heidi film yet, it is really to be highly recommended. It reminds one of everything that a better world would contain, of the value of real relationship and real relatedness, as I have wished and wish to have with you for example. The film brings back to memory what we once knew what was necessary, how important friendship, community, deep connectedness and yes, love is, because love used to be the yardstick by which everything was measured.

I wish you peace.

Friendly greetings to you

Samuel Widmer Nicolet

Appendix: Unfortunately still without...

a golden red sun redeems
a dying moon,
already almost new moon,
a good time to begin
completely anew
is it you, friend?

wedding

silent mist over the valley,
transparent veils plunge
all in pastel light,
with long drawn-out screams
the crows greet the young day
do I find you, my friend?

July 2016

Beloved friend,

You could say that the movement that we form is involved in healing. Involved in healing and becoming healthy, on the one hand; involved in being healthy and using that state of health to give birth to a new world, on the other hand. We want to write a new healthy, wholesome story. A mind in meditation is wholesome, a spirit blossoming in love.

When looking at the tools – community-making, psycholysis and Tantra – that we have named as supporting the process of self-knowledge and are using in practice, if you are somewhat familiar with us and the movement we thus belong to, you will realise that there is actually a fourth tool missing: the warrior training. We touched on it briefly in our 2nd newsletter of February 2016, mentioning dreaming, an aspect of warrior hood, as an ideal tool to unite people in a spiritual movement.

Warrior training[8] and its whole background – the teachings of Don Juan Matus and the Toltec warriors summarized and made available to us in the works of Carlos Castaneda and his comrades in arms, Florinda Donner

---

[8] For more exact orientation – besides the listed authors – refer also to my own books on the topic:

- Dr. med. Samuel Widmer Nicolet: Die Kriegertexte/ Die Kriegerschule, Das WorldWide Magic Movement als Meisterstück der Meisterklasse für Psycholytische Psychotherapie; Ba-

Grau and Taisha Abelar – do indeed play an important role in our lives and in the movement we belong to. We actually place the warrior lessons of Don Juan, just like the teachings of Krishnamurti that we have already mentioned in our second newsletter, on the same level as self-knowledge. We indeed use the insights of these two main teachers as a further means of schooling in the process of awakening and self-exploration, so that we could well place them on the same level as the other tools: community-making, psycholysis and Tantra. However, it seems more appropriate to us to assign them an additional higher level in our thinking and our conception of the world. The inputs we received from these two sources thus arise more frequently in my writings and offer a more elevated perspective. It is my and our concern to thank and honour our most important teachers in this way. As said before, the teachings of Krishnamurti as well as the warrior training of Don Juan should be put on the same identical level as self-knowledge. What these schools conveyed were not just tools to support self-knowledge and meditation, but rather pure self-knowledge.

In this seventh newsletter we want to turn to the second tool to further self-knowledge that was mentioned: psycholysis. Psycholysis too – maybe even more so than community-making – is something that strongly connects and keeps us together in the movement we are creating. It is also something that, just like community-making and Tantra, stands for love, the actual meaning and purpose, the goal of all self-knowledge. This cannot be emphasized enough, since in certain circles (scientific and hedonistic), which also deal with psycholysis, there is the danger of it becoming more and more lost that psycholysis stands for love. The psycholytic tools awaken us for love. They bring us an awakening for love.
Seen superficially, the truth, all fundamental insights and premises, can always be reduced to something seemingly quite simple. It often seems almost

sic Editions, 2010 [The Warrior Texts/ The Warrior School, The WorldWide Magic Movement as Masterpiece of the Master Course for Psycholytic Psychotherapy]
- Samuel Widmer Nicolet: Vom Weg mit Herz/ Die Essenz aus der Lehre des Don Juan/ Eine Würdigung des Werkes von Carlos Castaneda; Nachtschatten-Verlag, Solothurn, 2002 [About The Path with Heart/ The Essence of the Teachings of Don Juan/ A Tribute to the Work of Carlos Castaneda]

banal: it is about love. Love is the solution to everything. Psycholysis stands for love.

In reality, however, there is the greatest complexity behind such simple formulae. Their simpleness is based on the simplicity of what has fallen into place – on the dissolution of the complexity of the seemingly insoluble that they leave behind. However, they testify to the infinite diversity of life that remains a mystery in its unfathomability.

The psycholytic process is of course about overcoming unresolved feelings within us and processing the personal and collective past that has never been tidied up. It is about facing fears and thus leaving them behind, also about integrating all other feelings. All in all, psycholysis helps shake off the personal and collective story, expand one's consciousness and finally become healthy and whole. All this and much more is self-knowledge, is contained in self-knowledge. However, self-knowledge ultimately leads to the overcoming and dissolving of the self and thus to the awakening for love. That is the most important thing. This remains the most important thing. All else is contained, summarized and enclosed in this formulation.

To begin with, everyone becoming involved with psycholysis faces a vast inner confusion, a tremendous inner chaos. The contents that are uncovered and brought into consciousness, seem at first to be completely disordered and unclear. They seem to follow no logic, submit to no order, and seem to be completely individual and threatening in their complexity. We experience ourselves in the same exposed state of confusion that mankind is in. Only after long quiet contemplation of these contents does a supra-individual and comprehensible structure emerge, which has general validity. Gradually a clarification and thus an emptying takes place so that stillness can emerge and space be filled. All that is seen and understood follows the law of transformation and dissolves again back into a state of unity of everything.

Perhaps this is why, in the enormous process of psycholytic self-discovery, it is inevitable to initially mistake the path for the goal, to take the means to an end as the end itself. It seems, everyone who embarks on this path is for a time so taken by the beauty he encounters, that he loses sight of where he is ultimately headed for. Whether he learns to enjoy the use of the psycholytic substances themselves, the intensity of the music under their influence, or sees the contents of consciousness which continuously open up to him for a while as essential, as long as he is serious and honest, he will in the end withstand all temptation and step towards the light that outshines all of these. He may fall in love with his personal story for a while before realizing that its recapitulation is primarily intended to loosen the spell under which it has placed him already his whole life. He may be endlessly taken by the fascination of the collective unconscious, before realizing that beyond this sea of silent knowledge an even larger ocean, the ocean of oneness is calling and wants to welcome him. Without this arriving in love, without the fundamental transformation from the ego-centric personality to the open-hearted being-human, psycholysis would have no more meaning than a form of community-making that would never lead to the creating of community.

Well, we are already in the middle of describing the process of uncovering by which psycholysis – or rather its tools, the suitable substances – advances the process of self-discovery and discovery of worlds. But what is psycholysis really?

Psycholysis[9] is first and foremost a psychotherapeutic procedure that is supported by the administering of so-called consciousness-expanding substances. We understand psychotherapy in this context as an introduction to self-knowledge. Furthermore, similar to the process of community-making, psycholysis offers the possibility of experiencing oneness, both in groups and in relation to the Whole, and is thus suitable for cultural rituals that fuse movements together. For us, psycholysis is above all a support in the tantric process – which we will outline in our next newsletter – and thus the community-making process, for which Tantra is especially well suited. First and foremost, however, psycholysis helps to understand oneself and,

---

[9] For more specific information, refer to the following books:
- Samuel Widmer: Listening into the Heart of Things/ The Awakening of Love/ The Undesired Psychotherapy/ On MDMA and LSD; Basic Editions; 1997
- Samuel Widmer: Stell dir vor, Du wärst ein Stück Natur/ Von der Lust am Verbotenen; Basic Editions; 1995 [Imagine You Were a Piece of Nature/ About the Pleasure of the Forbidden]
- Dr. med. P. Samuel Widmer Nicolet: Wer heilt hat Recht/ Band 2/ Die Art des Kriegers; Basic Editions; 2010 [Who Heals is Right/ Vol. 2/ The Warrior's Art]
- Samuel Widmer Nicolet: Living Together/ Community and Community-Making; Basic India Editions, 2017

through this understanding, to ultimately go beyond oneself. The self-awareness and the resulting experience that we, like everything, are made of love, is the central point. Even psycholysis ultimately is no end in itself, as a beginner amongst psychonauts may think at first. It serves the process of unity. If it becomes the most important thing, which may temporarily happen, one has not really understood.

In this sense, it is not so much the actual psycholytic experience that is important, but rather its integration in everyday life. Insights bestowed upon us by the potency of psycholytic substances become lost again, if we do not implement and realize them in day-to-day life.

Little or nothing has yet been said about particular enlightenments during the process of self-knowledge; this will be reserved for later and hopefully more extensive writings. The aim at the moment is to briefly outline the tools of the movement that we form, and so give an overview of the most important issues for the movement and the goals it hopes to achieve with these tools.

Self-knowledge, as we have determined earlier, leads into meditation. As soon as the self dissolves in its own self-observation and thinking becomes still, the discipline of attention that self-knowledge generates transforms into a state of meditation. Psycholysis, or rather the psycholytic substances, support or awaken this state of meditation in us. We learn to become inwardly still, to become empty, and from within this state to look at everything that is happening inside and outside.

Meditation is absolute non-doing. A mind that can finally refrain from all reaction, that knows to act from out of non-doing, to function without entanglement with the past, which is not a reaction to a challenge, but rather a direct becoming-active of the challenge itself.

Meditation goes beyond everything we know and includes everything. Meditation is a blossoming in love. A state of pure attentiveness which knows bliss that cannot be put into words. Meditation is a progression in the realm of stillness. To live as a meditative spirit in the midst of the world, in the middle of the daily hustle, without separating oneself from the world, but instead looking at everything from out of this stillness, leads to a truly religious life that avoids nothing, excludes nothing, sees and understands everything and still remains unscathed by it. A spirit that is not entangled. In the world, but not of the world. A renunciation of everything that self and its thinking has produced. A renunciation that stems not from renewed thinking, but stems instead from pure awareness. This renunciation is true religion. The end of thinking, the end of all self-centeredness. A dying, a death from which a new, a religious, a meditative life arises. A wholesome life.

Do you know, beloved friend, how much beauty, how much peace, how much joy there is in having a pure heart? A loving heart? How much space and breadth inside? How much wholesomeness?

May awakening come to you

Samuel Widmer Nicolet

PS For those who are interested, there is no change or further development in the criminal investigation to which we have been subjected. However, an imminent storm is to be expected.

I include as an attachment my last – at least for now – letter of 13 June 2016 addressed to the leading prosecutor.

I was wrong about the time
and too early, too untimely,
departed.
Now I sit here
and have time.
Time from out of the space
of timelessness
to write you a message of love.

For a short time
to fall out of time,
is a happiness and a blessing.
All too quickly
time takes one again
as captured prisoner,
closes the space
to the eternal and to love.

10 June 2016

The Public Prosecutor's Office
To the attention of Mr Claudio Ravicini
Franziskanerhof
Barfüssergasse 28
P.O. Box 157

4502 Solothurn

Final Personal Questions

Dear Mr Ravicini

This time I will be brief. I think, I have already communicated to you everything I have to say or to ask, and I have also made sufficient effort to establish a relationship with you. You would not or could not accept my repeatedly declared readiness to co-operate and to disclose all facts about our activities and thus spare ourselves your costly and laborious search for evidence and the inevitable quarrels regarding medical secrecy. Therefore, this will be my last letter for the time being. Somehow, it is definitely your turn now. Especially after the Federal Supreme Court ruled on the issue of unsealing.

What has been confirmed to me along the way, is that our legal system, probably like all bureaucratic structures, is a relationless absurdity, an inhumane apparatus, which one should better not come into contact with.
Of course, I could tell you know about "Schellen Ursli", a movie that I recently watched with our children, and thus once more start on the importance of real relationships. But, so what?

Another film that I initially had no desire to watch, but which really made an impression on me, was the new film about the pubescent Anne Frank.

Why do certain scenes in this film remind me of the hair sampling process in the remand prison that you had us experience? And why do I ask myself while reading the commented issue of Hitler's "Mein Kampf" that was recently reissued, whether the book was kept under lock and key for the last seventy years, so that the new generation would not realize that the world still thinks the same way it thought at that time – and by no means just Hitler? Everyone just doing their job. During the hair sampling scene and the house search, exactly the same. That was our experience.

Should everyone who is just doing their job be tried in court, because they are not thinking authentically and judging independently without bias about what they are involved in doing? Should they be locked up as a danger to the public?

Years later, when everything has gone wrong as it did in Hitler's era, the job-doers are sometimes brought to justice, as we saw this year and last year with the ninety-year-olds during the holocaust court proceedings.

Does that not indicate the self-deception of a rotten und unjust society, to expect severe punishments after the fact, when something should have been said at the time it happened? But, what does it matter? As far as I am concerned, I have on every occasion while performing my job always followed the law of conscience, which in a healthy world should stand above all else. Have I thus fulfilled or violated the expectations of society?

Do you know, what is my impression of the whole story? That I had already been convicted the first day, when I met you, and that the whole criminal investigation and possible court proceedings would only be a formality. Though I did not get this impression from you personally – you are of course only doing your job – but from the "authorities" that are applying pressure from behind the scenes. And it is getting stronger with every shoddily justified decision that has been made until now, from the Magistrates' Court, to the High Court and finally the Federal Court. Am I therefore now paranoid?

In closing, a kind of "confession" that summarises my thoughts quite well and which I hope you will not hold against me, as it is by no means meant ironically:

I admit that I would have hidden Jews during the Third Reich. I confess that as a guard in Auschwitz I would have protested against the annihilation of the prisoners. I also concede that I would not have bowed to Gessler's hat and I admit that I feel absolutely committed to the Hippocratic oath.

But what I do deny is having administered dangerous drugs to patients that were entrusted to me, or having instigated others to do so, or having condoned such a thing under my direction and in my practice. Where I hold firm is that I consider psycholytic therapy to be the best remedy for psychologically ill people and that I do not leave my patients uninformed regarding that the erroneously and tragically forbidden substances are the best for this purpose. What they, my patients, then do with that information, I do not feel responsible and accountable for, even though, I have to admit, I cannot blame them for wanting to do what is right and appropriate.

I admit that I find the legislation around psycholytic substances absurd, cannot accept it, and that I advocate its abolition. However, I deny violating it.

But, so what? May fate be kind to you!

With kind regards

Samuel Widmer Nicolet

I have a heart,
I have a king's heart,
a hero's heart.
The largest heart,
writes a friend,
be mine,
a broken chieftain's heart,
says my darling.

Big heart,
sad heart:
"It doesn't beat well",
remarks
the thoughtful doctor.
It is my heart,
the common heart,
the heart of mankind.

August 2016
(written in May 2016)

Dear Tantrikas and friends of the movement,
who endeavour to renew the earth and mankind through self-knowledge,

Is it not difficult at times, amid all the nonsense that surrounds us, to nevertheless find and sustain a perspective, to still believe that one day there will be a change in mankind towards more love and compassion? A real change, triggered not by regulations or dictates, but rather through understanding and self-knowledge. To be awake and blessed with intelligence in the midst all the superficiality and confusion that surges around us, seems almost as a risk factor for melancholia and doom. For without meaning and perspective, which can really get lost at times, one can hardly escape the abyss of depression. Every psychotherapist can tell you a thing or two about that. Against such, even though understandable notions, the warrior has an appropriate recipe:

He creates his own mood. Even though he knows that this is the most difficult of all his endeavours, he nevertheless shows himself all the more persistent in accomplishing it.
Is enlightenment ultimately a result of one's own effort? Something you bring about by your own power? On the one hand, I would certainly agree with the warriors. The mood of the enlightened person ultimately comes

from his unyielding intent to self-knowledge. That reaching this "goal" finally also needs grace, is another story that it seems we will get to talk about much later.

Writing newsletters requires a certain amount of leisure and time for gestation. That is why my letters, at least in draft, are written a few months before their publication. This time, I am spending a week of vacation with Danièle in France, north of Provence near Grignan. It is the end of May and all the roses are blossoming. We will probably only send out these lines in August, when all the glorious blossoms have faded.

It is to the credit of the Toltec warriors to have summarized the process of self-knowledge in a few handy formulas or instructions: lose one's own self-importance; erase one's own personal history; assume responsibility for everything; use death as an advisor; put an end to one's thinking. And so on. Or simply: the warrior creates his own mood.

He, who follows these suggestions willingly and sincerely, will be readily invited to integrate all the feelings contained in self-knowledge, so that in the end, the grace will occur that enables him to establish the mood of enlightenment within.

When I came into contact with these ideas many years ago, I immediately realised the value and deep meaning of these guidelines and started to earnestly apply them to my life. For this is of course a prerequisite for the undertaking to succeed. Self-knowledge does not happen on its own. I often wonder about people, about friends and acquaintances, who had or have also received this message but do little or nothing serious with it and who do not realise it in their everyday life.

Krishnamurti showed us precisely how to end one's thinking in the process of self-knowledge. One of the most important steps on the path to the mood of a warrior: stopping the internal dialog. He taught us to be precise. But the problem is not only the constant thinking of the undisciplined human being, but paradoxically also the thoughtlessness that accompanies it. The fact that one remains superficial, defending against any real confrontation with one's own personal issues, never reflecting honestly and fundamentally on the really important things - above all else the great issues and deep problems of humanity – is just as much a hindrance to exact self-knowledge and a prospering humanity, as the superficial and constant chatter of our brains. Stopping one's thoughts and becoming truly still within includes both aspects: an end to shallow, unnecessary thinking through awareness within oneself and an ability to contemplate truly and deeply where it is needed.

But we actually wanted to talk about Tantra in this newsletter, about the third important and special tool alongside psycholysis and community-making, which serves our movement on its path to self-knowledge. Unfortunately, there is not much to say about Tantra as I explained in my recently published book[10] on this topic - nevertheless, over 300 pages in length. Tantra has to be experienced in order to be understood. Tantra wants to be lived.

I see Tantra as the process of awakening for and becoming conscious of the fact that all is one and made of love. It is like meditation a path where one ultimately becomes "aware of every blink of the eye" and discovers that it is precisely this comprehensive awareness that in essence constitutes the mood of enlightenment and mood of the warrior, since it ultimately leaves all emotions behind and remains centred in the realm of pure perception, of the one feeling.

Which, once again, brings us to love, love and compassion, the path to and the goal of the whole endeavour of self-knowledge. Because that is what Tantra is all about, love and compassion and not at all about lust or ecstasy, as many errant tantrikas may think, Even though lust and ecstasy are naturally enclosed in love and even brought to their climax. Lust and ecstasy, if pursued for their own sake, only generate a half-hearted enjoyment mingled with suffering and fear. In Tantra, as in all of life, lust and ecstasy may not take first place, not come before love, otherwise they degenerate into shallow pleasure. They are meant to be a by-product of love and compassion and will only reach their maximum in this secondary role. These reflections point us directly to one of the most important issues in the groundwork of self-knowledge, to which we will soon turn to, namely the human urge to mistake pleasure for love.

---

[10] Samuel Widmer Nicolet: ... jedes Lidschlags dir gewahr/ Tantra/ von der Liebe Lebenskunst; Basic Editions, 2016 [... aware of every blink of the eye/ Tantra/ Love's Art of Living]

But why and to what extent does Tantra now help on the path of self-knowl-edge?

On the one hand, for us, Tantra is community-making. Psycholysis and the sharing within the actual practice of community-making both serve this, for us central, instrument of community-making that we found in Tantra. In this sense, we experience psycholysis and sharing as subordinate and adjunct to Tantra. On the other hand, similar to the ritual possibilities of psycholysis, Tantra is a royal expression of community, a tool to promote and celebrate community. We understand Tantra as the preeminent community-making and community-maintaining process. It is the most powerful tool to promote the community-making process. In Tantra, relatedness in the community finds its most accomplished and most artistic expression. You could also regard Tantra as the religion of community as we understand it.

Though, at times, playing with enormous clouds, the sun with its warmth is still there most of the time helping us regenerate. We are still quite exhausted. A typical French landscape is to be found in the surrounding area. Holm oak and lots of flowering broom everywhere. Its fragrant smell fills the air. Lavender fields take turns with acres full of vines or peculiar little trees. First I took them for almond trees. At times there are also olive plantations or grain fields shining red with poppies. All in all, the landscape it wilder but also flatter than the typical Provence located more south. The lovely rolling hills are missing. Here it is everywhere either flat or mountainous. Yet everything is full of beauty moving you to tears.

The little village does not amount to much. Impressive is Grignan, the little town nearby. I must have never seen such a colossal fortress as the one enthroned above it. Very special, however, is that it is a town full of roses, of course, all flowering at the moment and enchanting us with their ever-present perfume. They are shining in many colours from all the house walls and are climbing up every masonry. Really lovely. Every moment here is a real hit. It is easy for the tantric awake spirit, nothing escapes it.

By describing the tools for self-knowledge – community-making, psycholysis and Tantra – we have taken another step regarding the meaning and purpose of such newsletters. As we defined in our first letter, it is our intention to outline the most important and fundamental concerns of the movement we are forming, and to also describe the tools with which we want to reach the goals that we are striving for. Already there we emphasized self-knowledge as our main tool for reaching our main goal, defined as the renewal of ourselves and of our world. To turn earth into a paradise, we wanted to accomplish nothing less. No wonder, perhaps, that with such high ambitions we sometimes struggle with depression, as soon as we are confronted with the actual state of us humans. But that is precisely what self-knowledge and Tantra intend: The impossible. The unreachable. The consummate being human. The mood of the warrior.

In the last three newsletters we focussed on the supporting tools, because these can serve the main tool of self-knowledge, with which it is ultimately possible for us to accomplish what we intend, as just described. Community-making, Tantra, psycholysis. However, these tools also express the objective in their own way, when we follow them to completion. Psycholysis eventually shows us *the deep dimensions of all being*, community-making inevitably leads us to *true community*, Tantra opens us for the *tantric visions of reality*. These three forms of unfolding in the target area of our efforts towards self-knowledge are what we intend to grapple with in our next three newsletters, so as then to finally arrive at a whole series of monthly letters covering the basic work of self-knowledge: what it is, what it is always about at the beginning, what is it always about in the future.

This groundwork supported by the said tools – psycholysis, Tantra and community-making – we also call True Psychotherapy. Avanti[11] (www.aerztegesellschaft-avanti.org), the International Medical Association for Alternative Psychiatry and Real Psychotherapy, which we established alongside the earlier mentioned World Wide Magic Movement (www.world-wide-magic-movement.org) and the Kirschblüte Community Movement, serves the movement that we form together by bringing our concerns into the world.

---

[11] Avanti has summarized its thoughts regarding this matter in a textbook on True Psychotherapy:
Avanti (Samuel Widmer Nicolet und Mitautoren): Echte Psychotherapie/ Ein Lehrbuch/ Anleitung zur Selbsterkenntnis als therapeutischer Prozess/ Eine Psychotherapie für eine neue Zeit; Basic Editions, 2013
[Avanti (Samuel Widmer Nicolet and co-authors): True Psychotherapy/ A Textbook/ A Guide to Self-Knowledge as Therapeutic Process/ A Psychotherapy for a New Era]

Amidst all the hopelessness, we insist on the mood and the optimism of the warrior, wanting the impossible, wanting the renewal of ourselves and thus mankind and the world to prevail.
What is Tantra?

Is it not our highest concern to make a world that manages to coexist peacefully, a humanity that has learned to share and has a vibrant interest in blossoming together in love? And is it not self-knowledge, the insight into one's self that will bring this about?
Community, intelligent community, is what humans are lacking.
Tantra.

Today we have been again driving through the wonderful landscape with some appropriate and dashing music and have visited some lovely small villages. These poppy fields! Their brightly shining red, even in the gentle violet of the awakening lavender. And all the manifold greens. All in harmony with each other. So much beauty, it really moves you to tears. To be aware of every blink of the eye! Full awareness until nothing but this remains. And along with it their most beautiful qualities: Love, compassion, beauty and ecstasy. That is Tantra. That is enlightenment.
It is a bit more windy and cooler today.

May you be blessed to establish the mood of the warrior within.

Samuel Widmer Nicolet

Japaratinga

Discontent in the house,
dishonourable the garbage.
Thoughtful faces
hardly find one another.
Does a song of farewell resound
or do sad eyes call?

The older the soul,
the more it sees only misery;
yet beauty without end
it recognizes too.
The fool thinks he determines his path;
the wise man sees himself determined by the path.

Quiet creaking in the bamboo grove,
warm evening light floods
through whispering fronds.
Endless rolls the sea.
Gliding black, high above,
noble birds in the wind.

September 2016

Dear friends,

In Buddhism and Hinduism one is familiar with the spiritual concept of karma. According to this idea every action has its effect according to the karmic law. These consequences do not necessarily take effect in the present life, they might also only manifest themselves in a future one.

The idea of karma is also strongly connected with the belief in reincarnation, another concept that assumes a chain of re-embodiments of the soul in diverse forms after their respective death.

Whether these concepts describe reality according to observations or are just dogmatic beliefs of these world religions, is something that everyone will have to examine and judge on their own. In any case, fact is that these conceptions are often misunderstood or have been oversimplified for the masses, so that they are then definitely no longer comprehensible, as is often the case with religious concepts.

True Psychotherapy, or rather transpersonal and psycholytic psychology, has, however, made similar discoveries but can also give the psychological explanation for these and for the psychological mechanism behind it.

As humans we tend to suppress, split off, or in some form repress the especially difficult feelings we have been exposed to during our development. As the result of this unlived life, the stored memories in the brain are shifted into the unconscious and their energies stored as an emotional package in the body. These packages ultimately result in the muscular and character armour described by Wilhelm Reich, including the insensitive dullness that hinders and ultimately almost completely blocks the free flow of energy, love and feelings in body and soul.

On the one hand, these stored emotional packages and their associated memories and images are usually well locked away, so that it is difficult to revive them by means of the usual talk therapy or other therapeutic methods. Here the psycholytic method then often helps with the process of uncovering, which is why it is advocated by True Psychotherapy. On the other hand, these memory packages are all about undissolved, unresolved sets of problems that by their nature are literally clamouring for dissolution or rather resolution. This presents itself in various symptoms, which conventional psychotherapies then endlessly attempt to treat without ever getting to the root of the problem. Symptom formation and the persistent variety of symptoms can be understood as a healthy response to an underlying malady, similar to pain when we hurt ourselves. Unfortunately, the symptom formation usually leads merely to an ever-recurring compulsive repetition, which is then often further maintained by a conventional therapy that endlessly multiplies and cultivates the symptoms instead of understanding them in terms of their message.

This is where psycholytic psychotherapy with its excellent tools, psycholysis and its substances, has its application. These support the urges of these forgotten energies and feelings that want to be recognized, lived through, understood and overcome. Only when all this is resolved and the individual concerned can again face the challenges of life in the here and now in a completely new and unneurotic manner, can tranquillity return. These unlived, unconsciously held and suppressed feelings push their way through symptom formation into manifestation in day-to-day life, into materialisation. Their suppression or non-suppression has implications. They most often produce massive consequences. You can often see how a whole life, an entire personality is controlled by these suppressed, unconscious states, how a destiny that wants to unfold in joy and love is thus corrupted into suffering, conflict and failure without this ever being understood.

Liberation from this inner burden and misery brings forth the solution. The karma that was created by the act of suppression transforms from a sluggish unfree constriction into a new liberated vitality which can once more be approached in innocence.

Similar to the Buddhist teaching of karma, we can also observe in the psycholytic dissolving process that such packages of feelings are often not merely personal. We then talk about opening up the collective unconsciousness and we experience in this process, how the collective guilt of the unresolved past controls and dominates our world, both personally and collectively, with even greater power. Karma.

It seems that in the process of liberation triggered by the psycholysis - which, as we have already noted in earlier letters, after some initial difficulties ultimately takes place according to a supra-individual pattern - every psychonaut is invited to immerse himself for a while in this pool of ancient pasts and carry away a part of the unresolved guilt of his ancestors. "The sins of the fathers shall be visited unto the third and fourth generation," or something similar, as already spoken in the Bible regarding this problem.

The unresolved packages of feelings do not seem to just simply dissolve when a human dies, but rather they continue to press from out of the collective pool, where they have been deposited, further towards resolution. Even from there they manifest themselves in severe symptoms, forming the basis of the suffering of entire peoples until someone is prepared to accept them, to take on their burden and hold the related feelings.

The reward of the warrior who takes on willingly what has been assigned to him, on the one hand, consists in really learning through this process to have compassion. On the other hand, the energy released by him eventually belongs to him. It is completely available to him, surrounds him in his life as free-flowing love and power.

Reincarnation is a possible explanation for such experiences. It may be that when delving into the collective pool we simply have to clean up, meaning recapitulate, what we have not looked at in our own fully-personal past life. Personally, I prefer the explanatory model where we all have access to a vast ocean of all collectively-lived experiences, and each one of us on our personal path to maturity is responsible for processing at least one impersonal part of this past. Apart from the fact that, by accepting this task, we individually free ourselves from being further controlled by this collective burden of guilt, we open ourselves to the Great, the impersonal and collective, and overcome the separation caused by the ego barrier and thus mature to finally experience selflessness and thus the unity of all.

Of course, for someone who has not himself progressed into such matters, even a psychological explanation of karma and reincarnation at best is nothing but a religious or spiritual belief. But that has been the crux with all religions. There has always been in their innermost a mystical core of genuine experience, but what was seen by the masses remained just an idea that could be believed or not believed.
Intuitive science demands proof through one's own experience, one's own emersion and comprehension. On the other hand, however, there is no need for external proof; the inner vision unlocks the truth to each seeker directly and without doubt.

In the last three newsletters we have dealt with the three tools – psycholysis, Tantra and community-making – that serve our movement as support in regard to self-knowledge, and now we are opening a new chapter in this and in the next two newsletters.
We perceive self-knowledge as the tool that will enable us humans to renew and transform ourselves and our world, so that it can become a paradise of love and compassion.
However, the mentioned tools for self-knowledge – psycholysis, Tantra, community-making – already contain this goal as a potential within themselves, point towards it, want to bring it to light or rather help us to substantiate our conception of a paradise of love and compassion. Psycholysis, or rather the psycholytic substances give us a glimpse into the *deep dimensions of our being*, Tantra opens us up for the *tantric vision* inherent in evolution, and community-making leads us, as long as we are earnest, inevitably to authentic and finally *true community*.
Before tackling in subsequent newsletters the many individual aspects of the groundwork regarding self-knowledge, we want to use the next three newsletters to take a look at the desired 'end result' of all self-knowledge by means of the perspectives granted by psycholysis, Tantra and community-making. Getting an initial overview of the whole thing and its wonderful possibilities may motivate you to enjoy the painstaking detail work at the foundation.

With the remarks about the concept of karma in this newsletter, we have already embarked on the journey into the deep dimensions of our being[12], which psycholysis helps us unlock. The insight into the collective unconsciousness and therefore also into the ocean of still knowledge is merely the beginning of this journey. As the warriors advise us: When we become very still, when we learn to stop our thoughts and thus the world, and as explained in our last letter, learn to think in an orderly way, which is equally important, a gate opens to us in this stillness of the moment, of the here and now, a gate that allows us a glimpse into the temporal dimension of all being. We learn to travel therein. We learn to *dream*, as the warriors also call it. The temporal dimension, as simple as it may seem to us because of its meaning in our day-to-day consciousness – past, present, future – is of all inner maps[13] that we psychonauts use in order to travel the threateningly unstructured realm of our inner being – layer model, energy system, Grof's perinatal matrixes etc. – surprisingly the most challenging. It requires us to already have a lot of free energy in order to move in any way freely with regard to the deep dimensions of past, present and future. By delving into the collective unconsciousness, we have already started. We have opened the door to the deep dimension of the past of our being.

However, another much more tremendous view reveals itself to us when the portal to the deep dimension of the present or even the future opens itself in us. In the deep layer of the present we find what is generally called shamanism. Clearly, not the hocus-pocus shamanism as Don Juan Matus described it, but actual *dreaming*. When looking into the future, we catch a

---

[12] More on this topic you can find for example in my book:
Samuel Widmer: Bis dass der Tod uns scheidet.../ Psycholyse/ Psycholytische Psychotherapie/ Die Geschichte der substanzunterstützten Psychotherapie in der Schweiz und in Europa nach 1970; Basic Editions, 2013 [Until Death Separates Us.../ Psycholysis.../ Psycholytic Psychotherapy/ The History of Substance Supported Psychotherapy in Switzerland and Europe after 1970]

[13] Further details on this particularly in:
Avanti (Samuel Widmer Nicolet und Mitautoren): Echte Psychotherapie/ Ein Lehrbuch/ Anleitung zur Selbsterkenntnis als therapeutischer Prozess/ Eine Psychotherapie für eine neue Zeit; Basic Editions, 2013 [Avanti (Samuel Widmer Nicolet and Co-Authors): True Psychotherapy/ A Textbook/ A Guide to Self-Knowledge as a Therapeutic Process/ A Psychotherapy for a New Age]

glimpse of the vision inherent in evolution, of the universal Spirit's intent, of the tantric visions for which Tantra then also stands.

However, it is pointless to even talk about these things. For those who have no access to it, these are merely words, tales of power, as the warriors call it, not acts of power. Yet precisely the latter are needed if our words are not to degenerate into an intellectual belief system, but instead echo throughout the universe as words of power. Just as already mentioned in relation to Tantra, one cannot really convey anything about these dimensions with words. Tantra, psycholysis and ultimately also community-making, and even more so the deep dimensions opened up by these approaches, are events that want to be and have to be experienced and lived. Words can at best only help people immersed in these experiences to exchange ideas, to communicate with other people who have committed themselves to the intuitive science. The experience itself cannot be conveyed.

Experience is the act needed in intuitive science. The act of power. Experience is the reality test, the verification of a result that another reports. One has to be engaged with Tantra, psycholysis, community-making and their deep dimensions in order to gain insight. No one who is not prepared to do so, can have the right to judge these disciplines. Being engaged cannot mean having had a one-off psycholytic experience or having visited one time a Tantra or community-making course. This may be enough to wake somebody up. To really understand and be entitled to an opinion, you will have to give your life for it. And even that on its own means nothing.

May you awaken for the deep dimensions of our being, dear friend.

Samuel Widmer Nicolet

PS: As far as the prosecutor's investigation is concerned, we are still waiting for a possible storm. Because of an article in the Solothurner Zeitung [Solothurn's Newspaper] of the 9th August 2016 by the anti-sect-warrior, Hugo Stamm, I felt once again determined, nevertheless, to write a few lines to the prosecutor, Mr Ravicini. I am adding them here.

As for us, we are of the same opinion as Leo Zeff, a psychiatrist and friend of the deceased empathogen researcher, Alexander Shulgin, that our obligation to help our patients must take precedence over the law. If there is a contradiction between the governing law and the possibility to help a patient, as a physician and healer I feel compelled to serve the patient and not the law. What is more, as defined by the last section of my letter, there cannot be anyone besides me or above me who can judge this. The duty to help a human being has to be above all other law, otherwise the current holocaust-convictions of over ninety-year-olds in Germany, who in those days failed to do this and are now being held responsible, would make no sense and obviously be a farce.

Ninaromina

No gentle tarantula
crawls over your belly and breast.
Where lingers now, my sweet Minne,
the tickle of our lust?

No snakes, no beasts,
oh, only sun, sea and sand!
What now, my dearest — don't look gloomy! —,
rescues our bond of love?

9 August 2016

Public Prosecutor's Office
To the Attention of Mr Claudio Ravicini
Franziskanerhof
Barfüssergasse 28
P.O. Box 157

4502 Solothurn

Regarding the article by Hugo Stamm in today's newspaper (9th August 2016)

Dear Mr Ravicini

Now, after all, I feel compelled by Hugo Stamm's article in the Solothurner Zeitung (9/8/2016) to briefly write to you again, even though I had expressed in June that I was going to refrain from doing so for the moment.

From the experiences I have had with you, I hope, I can assume that you have taken my questions and my statements not as a "frontal attack" on you or the prosecution, but rather understood them as an attempt to establish contact and clarification. Or am I mistaken there? In any case, I am sorry, if this should be distorted that way now. It was not meant like that at all.
I also assume that you, unlike Hugo Stamm, do not tend to use every sentence I write against me in such a way and to put it into such a distorted context in order to put me in a bad light again. Mr Stamm doing so is also the real reason, why I am no longer willing to talk with him.

That you often cannot take too seriously and too personal what is written in print media you probably know from your office just as much as I do.

Mr Stamm seems to have a real "sectish" interest in the matter. Unbiased framing seems to be something unknown to him. And this is being tolerated under "objective" journalism! He does not even list the source when quoting me (www.samuel-widmer.ch) since he obviously fears, readers could otherwise get a firsthand impression if they were to appreciate the overall context.

I am curious to see if Mr Eckert will show enough fairness to at least use my letter to you, of which he is receiving a copy, to counter the utterances of Mr Stamm.

Best regards

Samuel Widmer Nicolet

cc: Mr Eckert, Chief Editor of the Solothurner Zeitung

Glitter of sun everywhere.
Spring awakening!
Flowers, birds, even sparse butterflies.
The warmth expels the sickness,
that clung so tight,
out from the body.
Gurgling streams of water everywhere
in the light forest.
Not yet sprout the fresh leaves,
though frogspawn fills the pond
and here and there fidget
black shiny forms.
The great heron waits patiently.
Above all, stillness, expanse, space.
Life rejoices in all.
With evening
gradually descending,
melancholy stretches out its antennae
to like-minded hearts.

October 2016

Dear friend

To the psychological justification of the karmic law, which we have discussed last time, there is a supplement, which we had left out, as it is more suitable for the topic community than the topic psycholysis. There is actually another universal law that governs our access to joy, happiness, love and ecstasy. It is the law of ultimate justice.

As all beings, we strive to feel as much joy, happiness, love and ecstasy as possible. Normally we tend to "get" these states, meaning we make them dependent on others who should impart these to us by their presence and affection. Though in fact, the measure of joy, happiness, love and ecstasy, which we can enjoy in the end, depends on our ability to feel. Everyone receives exactly as much as they can allow inside themselves. This again depends on how blocked someone is, i.e., how many feelings one has rejected, suppressed and repressed inside during one's development period, and as a result, has to carry around unconsciously as muscular armour. This means, we are not only being "punished" by the accumulation of negative karma, meaning the blockage of the bliss-giving flow of energy as a result of many years of deeds of repression of feeling – but that we are also "rewarded" by our will to find self-knowledge, in that we can gain positive karma, the de-blocking of the energy flow within ourselves, and thus an abundance of ecstasy.

This means foremost that we are at all times fully responsible for how much suffering and frustration or respectively, how much happiness and love we are allowed to feel. You may be the Pope or the President of The United States; you are subject to this universal law of ultimate justice. If you are not ready or unable to allow this flow of universal nectar, you just will not get any. And for this allowing, you yourself alone are responsible.

But to be able to feel a great amount of joy, ecstasy, love and happiness, above all, also means to be able to give a lot of it, because without the vessel we form for this flow overflowing, it cannot grow into a strong stream. This brings us inevitably to the topic of greed, one of the main difficulties of mankind, which emerges out of their blockage, and which we will surely belabour soon in one of our newsletters concerning our groundwork of self-knowledge – and on the other hand – brings us to the topic of community as well, which we want to cover this time. For what would nourish the community more than the free exuberant flow of love between people?

The individual tragic you often encounter as a therapist, that the individual ability to feel in mostly socially well-integrated, completely "normal" people you treat is so limited that they can hardly feel anything anymore, Wilhelm Reich has described well enough. It is unbelievable how any access to devotion and the ability to be moved can be so lost, so that a person does not even have a clue that there is something sublime. How can between such individuals a true community ever come into bloom?

It may seem strange, when in the context of self-knowledge suddenly religious terms such as the law of karma emerge und are being discussed. Already in our last newsletter we indicated that we understand Tantra, which we use as a means for community building, as the religion of true community to some extent. Tantra is actually and originally a religious practice. It belongs to the mystical realm of Hinduism, the innermost circle as known by any alive religion and in which generally community is still blossoming.

Also in True Psychotherapy there is definitely a connection, or rather a naturally flowing transition, from self-knowledge (i.e. from psychotherapy as a guide to self-knowledge) and from psychology into spirituality and thus religion[14]. The term religion according to some etymologists supposedly stems

---

[14] Samuel Widmer Nicolet: Living Together/ Community and Community-Making; BasicIndia Edition, 2017

from the Latin verb "religare/religio" and is most often translated by spiritual seekers with "reconnecting", where sensibly a reconnecting with the source, the origin and the oneness of all is meant. (I will not get into the discussion of whether or not this is wrong or if rather the verbs "relegere" or "religere" were applicable here.) This makes sense but the connection with the goals of self-knowledge becomes even clearer – true community, tantric visions, deep dimensions of being – and their tools – community building, Tantra and psycholysis – which want to help them give birth and which we are dealing with at the moment, when we are thinking of a reconnecting, a reconnection directly with each other, directly amongst each other, a restoring of original community, the unity between human beings that we have lost.

But now in this newsletter, we want to especially deal with true community, the deep dimension of community building, this one tool we employ to support the process of self-knowledge. The deep dimension of psycholysis we have turned to in our last writing, the deep dimension of Tantra, the tantric visions we experience as inherent in evolution, we will give our attention to in the next newsletter. True community is the "goal" of self-knowledge that community-making strives for.

Community-making leads through a natural process of chaotic conflict-handling and finally emotional emptying, from pseudo-community conforming to a mutual feeling of connectedness or community as described in detail by Scott Peck, an American psychiatrist. Anyone who has ever experienced the intensity and simplicity of the process is taken by its beauty and convinced of the value and absolute necessity of community.

Even though this feeling of community can be reached quite easily in the sharing process of community-making, hardly anyone will fool themselves that the materialisation of such a feeling of unity, on which a lasting peace and decent form of living together could be based, is not so easily reached, but that for its formation a thorough self-knowledge and great willingness to cooperate is required in all participants. In a group of 50-200 people it may be successful over a period of years to form the quality of an authentic community which is able to overcome their conflicts gracefully. However, this only if these people can decide to actually live together, which generally already requires a lot of groundwork and a good portion of luck to even find the needed willingness. For mankind as a whole to find a way out of their pseudo-community hypocrisy and selfish separateness, which they have established for themselves and to find authentic conflict management and cooperation would already be a tremendous step.

However, the community-forming process aims at something even more encompassing. Its deep dimension is the true community in which finally all forces show themselves insightfully and have found a conflict-free cooperation, a life of being joyfully together and there for each other. In the book "Living Together", as already mentioned in the footnote, I have described such oneness in detail.

As already mentioned several times and also in the last newsletter regarding the deep dimensions of psycholysis, it is of little value though to lose too many words about that which could be but is not. Self-knowledge means to deal with reality, that which is and the going beyond in this process. To praise nice imaginations of what our life could look like in harmonious community, only brings about illusions which again will result in new conflicts and new chaos.

Honest and exact self-knowledge shows us eventually that all self-centeredness and egoism destroy the unity, disregard the wholeness and holiness of our oneness and are therefore responsible for all the separation and fragmentation present in man's world. The root of this separation is self-pity, which we humans love to indulge in. The warriors call it "the sheer insurmountable negligence of the human condition". Self-pity separates us, leaves us behind as something severed, abandoned and excluded. Out of this being excluded, which we love not, we then try to re-establish a connection by identifying ourselves with a thousand things, with possessions and possessing each other most of all, which causes additional division along with pain. Krishnamurti calls self-pity the darkness of dishonesty.

Self-knowledge and the meditation, which finally emerges from it as soon as self-knowledge has led to an inner order that allows inner silence, take a totally different path. They face that which is, reality, and thus overcome it. In the state of meditation the original and basic truth is regained, in which there is no separation, no I-consciousness. Self-knowledge and meditation reveal everything. All is uncovered in it; all is clear and finds its place and finds rest there. The madness of the world, which is trying to solve all problems through even more separation, even more control and oversized power structures, can relax again. Understanding, compassion and justice bring out in every terrorist or egotist their harmonic embeddedness in the All-encompassing.

With this little excursion into self-knowledge and meditation we are reaching ahead for what is soon to fill our letters, a closer look at the issues of self-knowledge, at their groundwork. But first, in our next, the eleventh newsletter, we will still cover the deep dimensions of Tantra, the tantric visions. These are no illusionary dreams or utopias of thinking, which are trying to bypass reality, but describe the universal intention, which is the foundation of all evolutionary processes and which we can fathom in our tantric or psycholytic future-focussed in-depth explorations.

In August this year, we, the Kirschblüte Community in Lüsslingen-Nennigkofen, offered and conducted a symposium on the subject of *Community*. As was the case so far at all our congresses, I was allowed to give the opening talk, which I conducted together with our son, Joshuan, this time on the topic "What do we want?" We will add our statements in the attachment. There also you will find a few thoughts on the feeling of unity that we all hunger for and on what the conditions could be to attain it together.

Delving into the deep dimensions of being – a process that goes together not with thinking but with great awareness, complete attention – also brings us back the ability to feel, which allows us to experience deep joy, great happiness, ultimate ecstasy and unending love. The stinginess, the reticence , one of the main problems of the ego-centrical human being, is shed from us and our senses open up full of surrender and the ability to experience anything they reveal to us as holy, unique and as a miracle.

May you awaken to the deep dimensions of our being, dear friend.

Samuel Widmer Nicolet

PS: For those interested in the further development of our legal proceedings: We are still waiting...

The last verse from the Samuel Gita[15], which I have promised our Indian friends for our Tantra seminar by the end of this year in Neredu Valley in India, and which may well be published as a little booklet, will give an idea of how we see things:

[15] Samuel-Shri-Prem-Avinash-Gita: Der Gesang des Begnadeten/ The Song of the Blessed One, von der unendlichen Liebe/ about love infinite, Basic Editions, 2017 (German/ English)

My artistry is
to skilfully bypass
the folly of your convention
without infringing against it
I am the Supreme Knowledge
I am beyond knowledge.
Also beyond consciousness
I am the Sacred, the Great.

Young souls – Old souls
(for Danièle)

Young souls know only one criterion,
by which they measure all:
Does it serve me? Does it bring well-being?
Is it about me?

Within, within this impertinence,
they meet with old souls,
to whom neither control nor convenience
have worth greater than freedom.

Both know the free flow of energy.
Old souls measure with more selfless standards:
How is it for you? Does it serve the Whole?
Does unity come from it?

When yet all control disappears,
when thus all energy flows freely,
it reveals itself in every case,
the unique that lies beyond all habit.

Young souls radiate it,
old souls swim in it.
Because all is open, all stability lost,
in the unstable the wonderful reveals itself.

What do we want?

Talk by Samuel Widmer Nicolet at the Symposium for Community hosted by the Kirschblüte Community in August 2016 in Lüsslingen/ Nennigkofen, Switzerland

As with each past congress or symposium, as our meeting on the subject of community is called this time, I have the honour to give the opening speech. Last year, on the subject of Tantra, I brought two of my daughters along, the two oldest of the Principi and Nicolet lineage, perhaps not so much to support me, but rather to express my impression that it is time for me to pass on the baton to the young generation, and above all, to point out how important the integration of each coming generation is for the blossoming of the community.
Therefore, this time I have asked Joshuan, the eldest son of the Nicolet clan, if he would like to do the greeting with me and help me out with a few lines of welcoming on the topic of "What do we want?" I will then add my own thoughts later on.

Talk by Joshuan:

So then, a hearty hello and welcome also from my side. So good to have you all here!

Originally, I wanted to keep out of the symposium and just remain on the sidelines by helping with organizational matters and the setting up and taking down of the tent. The reason being mainly that I don't really know what to say at this time and am pretty busy with my very own personal life, my relationships, my conflicts and my place in life. From time to time I really feel overburdened and worry whether I can manage life at all.
Now I have been asked personally to moderate after this talk and to guide us through the symposium, and in addition asked by my dear dad, to give the introduction together with him.
I was very happy about being asked and without giving it much thought I agreed straight away; only then to be faced immediately with the problem of not knowing what to do and feeling unworthy of the task.

But it is precisely this, here and now, that is community for me and this is the theme of this congress: community!

Community means relationship, thus the confrontation with oneself, the one next to you and the world. It means being in relationship with the network I live in and the creation of a strong, loving and stable field as a foundation, being able to advance into the endless and unfathomable mysteries of life, being held, cared for and kept safe, being able to open oneself up to the Whole without being overrun by it or blown away.
Therefore, community is the foundation for life, the basis for a pleasant and beautiful time on earth and the fertile ground for the mystery and spirituality, which next year's Congress for True Psychotherapy, Psycholysis and Alternative psychiatry will be dedicated to...

For all these reasons, this is here and now the right place for me. This is my family, here are my friends and the community where I'm at home. One is here with each other, sharing one's life with each other and right now I have the challenging task and beautiful honour of standing here with Samuel. Though my life at the moment is not so simple, it is nevertheless very beautiful and I can cope quite well.
The most important thing here for me is not that I have to do anything great and special, important and wonderful up on stage (that would be a nice side effect at best), but rather that I'm here because of the community, also for the community, and most of all with the community...
It's not about knowing or teaching anything, especially not on a topic such as community, or even in any other regard, rather it is about individually becoming conscious of one's relationship network, opening oneself up, understanding and recognising. To feel one's destiny therein, to accept it, to enjoy it and to love living for it.
Thus, a symposium with its strict structure, clear schedule of talks and breaks, is a delicate vessel for this topic and one has to pay attention that this structure, even though it brings us together, supports us and guides us, does not gain the upper hand and become too important, and that we do not lose the essential, the vital and the free, because then we'll miss out on life and true community.
For this is what we really want...
Of course, the vision of true community is now filling the air and one wonders what such a future could look like, what constitutes and binds together a group of people who earnestly face these questions and issues, what propels them forwards and where

are they headed. Yes, there have already been many widely different attempts towards community, wonderful and great things been accomplished, here with us and also in numerous communities around the world, without wanting to ignore the failures, the absurd, the perverse and the sick.

And yet, one could once again dare to try the completely new, to open oneself up for the unknown and to at least be ready for the unprecedented.

I experience it on a large scale in the world and in our community, and also on a small scale in my life: Basically one cannot plan anything, one has anyhow no idea how; one can with one's mind and intellect never come near the ultimate genius of life; and one is anyway stuck in that the future is constantly changing. Therefore, for me at the moment, it is the mood in which one pursues and spends one's life in that is more relevant.

There are difficult times, when one is heavily challenged, when there is much to do and to take, and times, when everything seems to take care of itself without doing anything at all.

Whether one is presently in the midst of a battle or one feels all light and celebrates life, whether one has to stand up for something or keep out or is currently not be in-volved at all , whether one is destined for something great, small, obvious or hidden, all this is secondary. Everything has to be covered, there are many different things to be done, exciting is merely in what mood I enter the stage, with what willingness and passion I play my role and how clean and nicely I step back into the background again. And, of course, also what I'm up to behind the stage...

When you can do this earnestly, immaculately and with joy, wherever you may be and whatever the conditions may be, then it is certainly good.

When one keeps all doors open, within oneself and one's relationships to others, with-out shutting oneself off from any possibility, and one meets life and its diversity with a basic willingness and is happy with all that is, then destiny and the future, no matter what it may look like, will be full of love, and a whole new vision will materialize, manifold and magnificent, indescribable in words.

Truly, the vision of love, the vision of community...

So then, thank you and I'll pass back to Samuel...

Surely, you must already have heard of the miracle of Pentecost. In the Acts of the Apostles in the Christian bible, chapter 2, verse 1-13, Luke gives an account of it. He tells us, how the Holy Spirit descended on those gathered together for the community-experience, so that they could all comprehend each other, even though they were conversing in different languages. The Holy Spirit was poured out upon them so they became one, one heart and one soul, just as Jesus had promised his disciples, as described in Matthew 18.20, "For where two or three are gathered together in my name , I am in the midst of them." What had happened? What is it talking about?

Isn't what is happening to us today, when we gather together to talk and – after a tough struggle with pseudo-community and working through the chaos phase and emptiness phase of authentic community – finally break through into the feeling of community?

What drives us when we gather together here? What do we want? Isn't it the hunger for this feeling of community? For the experience of unity? This is what we are all searching for, consciously or often also unconsciously. We want to be loved. We want to love. We want to feel united in a field of love. We are longing for it and we know at the same time how difficult it is to realize this state of oneness together. We can't find the entrance to it, we go astray, get on the wrong track and isolate ourselves, and yet still we can't help but hope for it. We wish for it on the small scale, we wish for it on the large scale: One world, united in peace, happiness and love, in a completely whole new story – whether openly acknowledged or otherwise – this is our vision. Being ridiculed, not taken seriously, being defamed – is part of it. The followers of Jesus didn't fare any better. They were ridiculed, as reported by Luke. "They are full of young wine," insinuated the uninitiated. For even though all are looking for unity, most don't believe it can be found. They are afraid of it. Afraid of the compelling consequences that result from it. Of the inevitable involvement. And they don't dare take the necessary steps to make it possible. Rather they try to prove that such a thing cannot exist by fighting anything that smells of love.

When we gather together here, we are searching for community, the community experience, a community feeling. We don't want to lose sight of it, as Joshuan already emphasized, during what we intend here together. This is the essential, what it's all about. With all the theories we may look at, with all the paths of healing to get there and all that we are inspired about, with all the disagreements in regard to the right approach, we don't want to forget that most of all we want to experience common happiness, a feeling of being cared for, even love. We want to experience community with joy and not just debate about it with our heads.

What is needed for that? And how deep do we want to go into it? These seem to be the questions we should therefore ask ourselves.

Two things are needed here. Firstly, a willingness towards honest self-knowledge, a passionate readiness to understand oneself thoroughly, and most of all, to also show oneself to each other. And secondly, it needs a willingness to come together, at the same moment, in the same place, with the same passion, with a common intention, a willingness to really listen to each other, understand each other, love one other. It is necessary for us to get together here in the name of love.

If need be, we use aids that have proven their worth, especially sharing together in various forms, but also tantric processes or deep psycholytic experiences. It is not so important which support structures we use, more important is rather the openness for each other, the honesty towards oneself and others, the impartiality that we employ of really wanting to know.

If there is willingness to face oneself and each other honestly, then the community feeling – the Pentecost experience – will invariably happen as soon as we sit down together with this common focus. And we know that this does not merely promise the solution for our individual problems and finding our individual happiness, but rather, and most important of all, it also contains a solution for any difficulty between people on a small scale and on the large scale in regard to the immense challenges in our world.

It is the sorrow of all awakened people that there are so few that can be won over to it; that most people would rather laugh about it. And that's why it is our unrelenting endeavour to awaken mankind for it.

What is needed therefore, is something very simple, something given to us naturally, for which we don't need any preparation or training: Honest, alert and unbiased looking; listening and feeling in ourselves and each other. It needs empathy. What is needed is that we gather here in the name of love.

Once this is clear, we can turn to the second question leading us even deeper: How deep do we want to go? And do we even have an influence on it?

Do we intend to be of one spirit as the followers of Jesus found in the miracle of Pentecost? Or do we content ourselves with being of one heart, which is the most that authentic community can achieve? Does it perhaps suffice us already to compare notes on the level of the will, the solar; to set opinion against opinion and to work on that?

Maybe we have little influence on how deep we can go together. For this depends on how far every single one of us has personally advanced in the perception of reality within the process of self-knowledge. Our status in this regard will be directly expressed in the result we can achieve.

To set opinion against opinion in order to gain consensus, is the level of the *pseudo-community*. There is still a lack of honesty, of true realization of how one's own self functions. It's the level of peace talks. The world of man is full of it. It lacks inner stillness, inner order. A meagre feeling of community that will leave our hearts yet empty!

Will we stagnate here, unable to go further because we still fulfil too few of the requirements needed to delve deeper, because we have cared too little about what is needed!

Or will we find connectedness in the one heart? The first gleam of a real community feeling! We will not feel completely one, but we will feel warmly connected. The not yet fully satiated hunger will be our yearning within. That would be the state of *authentic community*, where one no longer struggles with opinions but rather with the feelings that are caused by this struggle. Do we already have the maturity, the inner discipline of awareness, the wakeful attention for everything that's happening in us and in others, which grows out of earnest self-knowledge, to have this connectedness of heart between us come alive? Being aware of each blink of the eye! Exactly that which we acquire in the tantric and psycholytic process.

Or will it be possible for us in the next few days to allow the Universal Spirit to come over us, the intelligence of the Whole to enlighten us? Will the miracle of Pentecost be given to us, because we have created the preconditions for it within us? Because we are gathered here in the name of love? That would be the state of *true community*, of being together completely without conflict, wherein all feelings have been overcome, where everyone is in agreement because they recognise the same thing, perceive from the same depth, because they are of one spirit. Then we would be fully awakened human beings. People, who have completed the process of being honest with themselves and each other to the very end. Enlightened ones, who consequently go beyond all feelings, able to leave all self-centeredness behind. Who can open themselves up for the Great, the truly Common, for the realm of ultimate reality.

To hope this far might be presumptuous. This uniqueness will happen all on its own, where two or three are really gathered together in the name of the Immensity that is our home.
It might better to assume that we'll still have to "work" on it, that we must – or may – still further prepare for it.

"Perhaps we should talk about love once again," I once said to everyone at a community evening as a reminder of the correct work attitude.
What really is love? What do we mistake for love that may not be love at all? How do we recognize love?
Isn't it surprising that amongst those who are genuinely interested in community, there are many who believe that true community is attainable and is coming, even though on a daily basis they do anything else except love or live according to love?
Self-knowledge, honest self-knowledge, leads via the dissolution of self finally to meditation. Self-knowledge is the beginning of meditation. Meditation is the stillness of a mind that has created order in itself and can thus be still. In the state of meditation the gateway to love opens. To this essence of oneness that keeps the whole universe going. The gateway to the inexplicable. This Pentecostal experience happens in the aloneness of individual meditation. That it could become a united experience, as many individuals touch the same depth at the same moment with the same intensity and focused toward the same, the common, would be the miracle of Pentecost.
May it be granted to us.
Perhaps we really don't have a direct influence on how deep we can go together. Probably it is really presupposed and predetermined by how our consciousness is currently conditioned. In the long run we can unfold ourselves in this regard by learning to be aware of each blink of the eye, but for the time being, we have to accept things the way they are.

What we can do, however, is align our intention with the very best, gift our yearning to the highest humanly possible. What we really desire, what all humans hope for, is true community. Authentic struggle with each other or even pseudo-community arguing is not enough. It does not make us happy. That's my invitation to you during the next few days – our invitation to you to what we really want: To gather together here in the name of love. And that means: Together with us to strive for the most perfect, the unreachable, not to be satisfied with the mediocre, as genuine heart-warriors each in turn to demand the best of each other.

The simple
(for Marianne)

The simple is the best,
like fluttering butterflies,
like buzzing hummingbirds
and all the wondrous things.

The very special celebration
is found in the very mundane,
that touches without hubris
the very unique.

Sunrise emblazes you,
the wide sea longs to enthrone you,
the high heaven yearns to crown you.
How beautiful is the earth!

Rustling leaves, the end of the day,
swaying branches,
the evening slips into the calm
that is the heritage of beauty.

NEWSLETTER 11:
TANTRIC VISIONS

November 2016

Dear friend

At this year's Entheo-Science congress in Berlin, at which I wasn't even present, the various currents of the movement we form together met together and distanced themselves from each other. In the appendix you will find the very fitting final statement in the podium discussion made by Christoph Kahse[16], which will certainly be enlightening for understanding the underlying problem.

As for me, I have always welcomed the legalization efforts made by the scientific sector of psycholysis and found them necessary. But I am also more and more uncertain if it would indeed be desirable and helpful for psycholytica to be administrated by psychiatrists and scientists. They actually belong back in the hands of all mankind, in the bosom of humanity's cultural heritage known as shamanism. Increasingly with time, it seems to me that it is the termination of the war against drugs in its totality that is important, not their integration within conventional medicine as a partial strategy in this war. The denial of love and its revolutionary force in this process of reinstating basic human rights, seems to me just as dangerous as the earlier proselytizing and Christianization of the world's population – allegedly in the name of love – whereby that which is vibrant and has grown up naturally is

---

[16] Entheo-Science, Podium Discussion 2016, Berlin

first vilified and destroyed, in order to later propagate conformed niceness in its place. An interesting article by Charles Eisenstein also discusses this brilliantly[17].

In attempts to differentiate themselves from one another, the feeling of being excluded is pushed back and forth between the different groups and their representatives. One of us humans' favourite occupations: The other one should feel what I do not want to feel. No one wants to have the feeling of being excluded. As soon as a person accepts this feeling, he becomes a black hole of sorts. Since, through his being in agreement, he himself falls through all that is unwanted into the deeper dimension of love, he pulls everything that comes close to him along with him into the depths. Even though maybe struggling and resisting – everything crossing the event horizon cannot help but circle around that gravitational pull. In this way, the most unloved and most excluded person becomes the centre of the movement, the one with whom you always have to deal, even though you do not want to have anything to do with him.

This is an exemplary illustration of the path of self-knowledge that we want to describe starting with the next, the 12th, newsletter: Everything is held, guided and attracted by the Innermost even if everyone tries to escape it.

But in this 11th newsletter, we first want to outline the deep dimension of Tantra, the "goals" of self-knowledge, as given birth by the tantric process. These are the same tantric visions that are also revealed when we fathom the deep dimensions in the psycholytic process with regard to future orientation.

With this letter, we come to the end of what we planned to do first of all within the newsletters, namely to describe the most important and underlying concerns of the movement we form, and to capture anew its goals and also the tools for reaching those goals.

We defined self-knowledge – which after its maturation flows into the process of meditation – as our main tool, and understood community-making, psycholysis and Tantra as our most suitable aids on its path.

We have also turned our attention to the "goals", if such can be defined at all, that the path of self-knowledge and meditation "aims at", to the deep

---

¹⁷ Charles Eisenstein: Psychedelics and Systems Change, MAPS Bulletin, Summer 2016

dimensions of psycholysis and to true community that ultimately wants to
grow out of community-making.

Today we conclude this extensive description with a few elaborations concerning the tantric visions that Tantra wants to bring into the light of our consciousness.

With that, the way is then clear to devoting ourselves – commencing with the twelfth newsletter – to what we consider the most essential content of our movement, the actual exact and honest self-knowledge, which forms the bedrock for all the blossoms we describe and for the existence of our movement.

On our way, I hope, at least two things should have become clear through these introductory letters:

- Firstly, we are in truth not at all a movement. We only use the term, because we have not found a better one. However, we actually mean it differently than it is generally understood. In the process of self-knowledge, it quickly becomes clear that in order to face reality, we have to stand alone. To grasp what really is and thus go beyond it, we have no choice but to disassociate ourselves from every affiliation and stand outside of everything. Seen like that, we are maybe, if such a thing can exist at all, a movement of outsiders. To free oneself from old and untrue patterns of thinking and acting, one has to part with every form of community, all affiliation to groups, any religion and societal morality. Only when standing completely alone is real cooperation, true compassion and with that true community, and real working together possible. For that, standing beyond all the corrupted conditioning and structures of habit of the past and of the human society, standing as an outsider, is the beginning. In the next newsletters it will become clear to us that out of this process of detachment, out of the courage to disentangle yourself from all that is false, is born precisely that path of self-knowledge which confronts us with all those rejected feelings, whose integration actually constitutes self-knowledge. Seeing that which is, means facing up to precisely these feelings of powerlessness, of loneliness, of being excluded, and thereby going beyond them in meditation into the ecstasy, joy and love of being alone and thereby being One.

- Secondly, when we look out for tantric visions today, we are - as hopefully it will have become clear to everyone by now - for the lack of a better alternative, using a term that usually describes something utopian or illusionary. But in this context, this is not the manner in which we are using the term "visions". We are, on the contrary, using it to outline something that in the process of self-knowledge and meditation crystallizes as the truth, the ultimate truth even. The aids to self-knowledge to which we have dedicated ourselves support us in this. In the process of community building, ultimately the possibility of true community presents itself to us. Besides the view into the collective unconsciousness via the path into the past, and the plunging into the shamanistic deeper dimensions of our being via the broadening of the present moment into the eternal, psycholysis also gives us an outlook into that which is coming via its future dimension. This outlook is free from the over-enthusiastic and illusionary content created by thought. It is a direct perception of what is, and in its profoundness, ultimately an outlook beyond the rim of the mundane into a depth or breadth that lets us divine that which fate determines. It is not about foretelling the future or about specific prophecies, but rather about an understanding, about a general overview over the workings of the forces of fate, in regards to the personal, or rather the collective, even the universal life and consciousness. It is a matter of connecting into the universal purpose that reveals itself more and more in that the self-will is overcome. It is through the subordination of the self that the will of the Whole, the purpose of evolution, the "goal" of universal intelligence reveals itself to the consciousness. The impacts and prospects of such on our living together as humans are what we call tantric visions.

With this description of the term, we have already ventured out far into what we want to relate concerning the deeper dimensions of Tantra. The same applies here again in that all description is actually futile, since words originate from thinking, but we are concerning ourselves with a dimension of being that really cannot be reached by words. So once again, it can only be about pointing towards a magnificent possibility for us humans, the possibility of a wonderful awakening. Everyone who feels invited, will have to walk the path alone. That is the reason why we are not really a movement, which is understood usually as a synchronisation of thinking, but rather purely outsiders standing alone, who have, out of their being alone and being one, finally latched into the movement of the Whole – the movement of the universal intelligence and of love – into the true and the only "movement" that can move something fundamentally new, that can move into a completely new story

Why do we call the "visions" that are coming out of this "divine" view, tantric?

Probably, mainly because they manifest themselves even more clearly in a combination of Tantra and psycholysis than they do through engagement in community building or psycholysis alone, or in combination of these two. In the process of self-knowledge, it is often only the tool of Tantra that brings out the very tenacious conditioning of wanting to possess each other and the associated feelings that are very difficult to integrate.

We often see that experienced psycholytic practitioners and seasoned community experts find themselves once again left massively reeling in the tantric process, as they begin to confront in the area of relationships the patterns in which we are caught and the basic freedom to break through them, for themselves and, above all, allowing the same for their partners.

It is no coincidence that we see the tendency to split that had already emerged thousands of years ago as the red and the white line in the original Tantra, showing up again in our movement. The honourable psycholytic practitioners, who aspire for enlightenment only above the waist, are split from the wicked tantrics, for whom enlightenment begins in the pelvis[18]. Whereas the latter also want to experience the red freedom in the body, in the pelvis, in the material world, the former think they can restrict themselves to the white sublimity of the head level. That the tantrics like to lose themselves here in the wrangling of relationship conflicts and therefore never get to see the light, is then willingly taken by the ones adept at psycholytic enlightenment as proof of the correctness of their one-sided orientation, without

---

[18] More about this can be found, for example, in this book:
Samuel Widmer Nicolet: Essenz schauen/ Vom Ruhen im Urgrund des Seins/ Die Spiritualität beginnt im Becken/ Ein Buch über Freundschaft und Esoterik; Basic Editions, 1998 [Looking at the Essence/ About resting at the very base of all being – Spirituality begins in the pelvis/ A book on esoterics and friendship]

them ever honestly facing the fact that their white light in the head is also merely a thought construct, since they are simply lacking the red force of the pelvis that has freed itself up into the heart and head, which is necessary for real illumination. Enlightenment really does begin in the pelvis.

That is also why it seems to suggest itself, that those visions that reach far beyond sexuality should be described as tantric. Because repeatedly, even in tantrically interested people, the tendency is still huge whilst striving for enlightenment to try and cheat around the topics of possession in general, and specifically the possession of each other in relationships, in sexuality. This issue still seems to be – of course, alongside the sharing of material goods – the most difficult one on the path of self-knowledge.

But then what do we see when the Great Spirit blesses us in moments of enlightenment giving us a glimpse into the future of evolution, or even just our personal unfolding of potential?

As I said, to speculate about it would really just lead us into illusionary thought-constructs. It is this very thinking, however, that denies us access to these deep dimensions. It must be overcome and assuaged in the process of self-knowledge before the door to the Great opens, before the fully great insight can fulfil us. Therefore, it is much more important from the next letters onward to recapitulate what self-knowledge actually is, to start again from scratch and to walk the individual stations of this path. The grace of meditation will then come to us by itself, if we have conscientiously attended to it.

Nevertheless, in conclusion, a few words about what is shown to us there in an individual manner, and yet is as always the same[19].

It is the realm of love, the possibility of love lived, of love lived in all the areas of being. Whether this is described as True community, as tantric vision, or as the ultimate reality of meditative experience of unity – it is always about the same and cannot be conveyed with words. If you want to smell

---

[19] Further illuminations can be found in:

Samuel Widmer Nicolet mit Marianne Principi: ... jedes Lidschlags dir gewahr: Tantra/ von der Liebe Lebenskunst; Basic Editions, 2016 [Samuel Widmer Nicolet with Marianne Principi: ... aware of each blink of the eye/ Tantra/ a textbook/ about love's art of living]

that scent, taste that delicious taste, you will have to set out on the path that we will start talking about next time. There is only one's own experience on the path of self-knowledge, only personal aloneness, the individual awakening for the realm of love. Descriptions of it may sometimes encourage us, lure us, but their stimulus does not go far. Even though the light ultimately comes to us as grace, it first of all takes our own perseverance – a deep yearning to want to see the light that must drive us – otherwise we will never be able to end the imprisonment in the known, the old, the habitual. Krishnamurti, like no other, has left us with descriptions that can awaken this yearning in us. Therefore, I would like to conclude with a small section from a recently republished book[20]. In the text he describes the miracle of meditation for which self-knowledge ultimately opens you up – when you follow this path to the end – and with it, the movement that we have really committed ourselves to.

Meditation is a never-ending movement. You can never say that you are meditating or set aside a period for meditation. It isn't at your command. Its benediction doesn't come to you because you lead a systematized life or follow a particular routine or morality. It comes only when your heart is really open. Not opened by the key of thought, not made safe by the intellect, but when it is as open as the skies without a cloud; then it comes without your knowing, without your invitation. But you can never guard it, keep it, worship it. If you try, it will never come again: do what you will, it will avoid you. In meditation, you are not important, you have no place in it; the beauty of it is not you, but in itself. And to this you can add nothing. Don't look out of the window hoping to catch it unawares, or sit in a darkened room waiting for it; it comes only when you are not there at all, and its bliss has no continuity.

May you wake up to the tantric visions that our being contains, dear friend

Samuel Widmer Nicolet

---

[20] Jiddu Krishnamurti: The Only Revolution – meditations on interior change; Victor Gollancz Ltd., 1970

PS: There is little to report on the criminal proceedings, which are still pending. In a crime novel given to me on vacation, I found this beautiful phrase that also applies quite well to us:

"... whatever we are up to might be dubious in the eyes of the law, but not a crime against God's laws"

Appendix: A Plea for Love (by Christoph Kahse)

Death

Thrice you have already touched me,
yet thrice I have escaped you.
You bring magic, when not the end,
a change towards the Great.
From the wondrous is spun
your due and your kingdom.

Your strike creates the thin thread,
on which the great things hang.
Only he who loves you becomes free from fear,
close to the abyss, he lives the longest.
With powerlessness you know how to urge us,
'til inexistence becomes pure power.

A Plea for Love

A contribution to the panel discussion
Entheo-Science Congress Berlin, 2016

By Christoph Kahse
German Psychedelic Society

I guess I am supposed to present a rousing polemic speech at this point and show everyone what stuff I am made of. But actually, I am one thing above all else, and that is sad.

Actually, I am filled with grief over a glaring rift in the psycholytic movement, whose original matter of the heart in the early days of the SÄPT, I can feel astonishingly well, even though I was not even involved.

In the German part of the very diverse psycholytic movement there are, I think, two major points of tension: The scientists around Peter Gasser and those in the underground around Samuel Widmer. When I immersed myself deeper into this debate some time ago, I noticed with shock that this division has already continued into the next generation of those interested in psycholysis on both sides. The science section consider themselves nowadays to be the naturally most appropriate caste, preordained for the effective handling of psycholysis. Their slightly smug arrogance is of course not hidden, nor the underlying pursuit of elitist sovereignty over the interpretation of anything psychedelic.

And of course, the people of the Widmer scene are also affected by this Ingroup-Outgroup-bias. For where there is a "WE HERE", there is always also a "THEM THERE". Such divisions are in substance just as debilitating as they are human and they also bring interesting confrontations with them, which we have to face.

Again and again at this congress, the revolutionary potential of the psychedelics flared up. Again and again the issue is a conflict between the conformist middle-class values of this society and the non-conformist insights we gain with psychedelics.

The researchers concern themselves – this is to be welcomed – with the approval of psycholysis for the treatment of mental disorders. At the same time, they rigorously dissociate themselves from less conformist, and also broader, perspectives that do not fit into the usual psychotherapeutic consensus reality. They want to subscribe psycholysis as exclusively as possible to this limited field of application. And the revolutionary potential of psycholysis - the magical, the ingenious and the innocent - is played down to suit this purpose or even denied. Perhaps this stems from a limited view of our reality, perhaps it is the hypocritical attempt to sell to the bourgeois and established forces in society a revolution of consciousness filled in harmless pudding cups. But perhaps there is something else behind it.

Psycholysis is anyway already a controversial issue. He, who engages with the subject of "drugs in therapy", comes inevitably in contact with feelings of exclusion. He, who mentions "psycholysis", is out! And he, who mentions "Samuel Widmer", is straightaway completely out! Is the old game repeating itself here? In society today, it is also often still a stigma to go to a psychotherapist. And in the psycholysis scene, there is something wrong with someone if he likes Widmer. To be associated with the Widmer scene is as attractive for some here as the idea of swallowing LSD is for a conformist bourgeois. But avoiding the difficult feelings of exclusion only brings additional conflict, and no integration - in other words, the inherent human striving for wholeness of which Simon spoke yesterday. The rigid attempts of the scientists to delimit themselves arise from the attempt to place their own exclusion into the lap of the underground and its representatives. Thus, the underground represents science's shadow: What one defends oneself against, one gets again in the end, but presented with much more force. But from what should or must one now actually distance oneself? Is research representing seriousness on the right track, and is the underground as charlatan running astray? Does research merely represent an anxious conforming to a system that is sick and the underground stand for true freedom? I guess it's not that simple. We humans often tend to make superficial simplifications when we don't see the depth of a situation. And anyway, the dividing line for seriousness runs along a different line. Because even if psycholysis can be extremely helpful in therapy, psychotherapeutic use is only a small part of the entire serious spectrum of psycholytic possibilities.

Research thrives on discourse. But if you don't talk to each other, the rift will continue to widen. So: let's do psycholysis. Let's shift the focus away from the well-known participants and deal more with our inner self. Let's integrate being excluded!

Then the space of love behind it opens up. And love is a rebellious force. It is neither a violent reaction in the form of revolution, nor a shallow cuddle-seminar. Love is an authentic and honest rebellion against falsehood and denial.

If we give leadership to the heart inside ourselves, closely followed by the head, if psycholysis again becomes a collective matter of the heart, then unity can come about. Then a force can unfold that tears down the Berlin Wall. If it is the other way around, there is only conflict.

In my opinion, this is the essence for which psycholysis can actually awaken us.

Part II: The Groundwork of Self-knowledge

The spirit trapped in the body —
Does consciousness ever fly free?
The soul veiled in fate —
Is freedom mere illusion?

NEWSLETTER 12:
THE INDIVIDUAL STEPS WITHIN SELF-KNOWLEDGE

December 2016

Dear friend of the self-knowledge movement,

The Year of Foretold Promise that we talked about at the beginning of this year is coming to an end. We had announced it with a sense of humour, almost carelessly, at our Christmas meeting twelve months ago at the end of the Year of Decline in 2015. At that time we did not really know what the foretold promise might be and yet in the meantime it has become clear to us that we had not understood this correctly at the beginning. Last year we mistakenly looked out for what could have been promised and should now come true. But this would then have been the Year of Fulfilment, which, as far as we can see, will only come in two or three years' time. No, only in the Year of Promise Foretold did it become clear that a fulfilment was even promised. And this has ultimately carried us through the year.
We expect next year to be the Year of Clarification.

In the first eleven newsletters we have tried to make clear what the movement we form is all about, to what extent we form a movement or not, what the concerns and aims of this movement actually are, and what tools and other means of support it uses to achieve them.
Commencing with this twelfth newsletter, we want to turn our attention to the main tool to which we are committed, namely self-knowledge, and

examine in detail what self-knowledge actually means and how to apply it productively.

What exactly is self-knowledge?
Self-knowledge is quite simply the intention to see and understand one's own behaviour, one's reactions to external or internal events, one's attitudes and beliefs, especially one's own thoughts, one's whole inner life and its expression externally and in our relationships. In particular, self-knowledge is concerned with fathoming out the background that feeds this inner life and its external expression. Self-knowledge is taking stock of one's own internal inventory.
It is important to take a very close look, an unbiased and honest view, to employ a very precise method. Without great honesty, a total willingness for truth, one will not get very far on this path. It is about the "sincerity of the intention to be honest towards oneself" or "intellectual honesty" as Thomas Metzinger in his well worth reading essay[21] by the same name calls it, or rather in which he quotes Immanuel Kant.
The "aims" that we formulated for self-knowledge initially play no role whatsoever in this process. Actually, these are not aims at all, but rather that which ultimately emerges as a simple and natural result of this process. Self-knowledge is sought for its own sake, for the sake of the truth for which it stands. The fact that it additionally also produces something fruitful, just like a tree bears fruit, happens in a completely natural way and is of small concern. What drives us to engage in self-knowledge is precisely this passionate interest in truth, in reality, that is necessary for it. An urge to simply want to know and understand what is, what something is, how we function psychologically.

We humans like to delude ourselves. We construct images of ourselves that please us. We like to rationalize possible wrong behaviour. We have a great ability to manipulate reality and to twist everything in such a way that it finally fits into how we imagine ourselves and the world. The adept of self-knowledge sees this tendency in us, the lying and distortion, and consciously opposes it with his contrary directed interest. He is driven by

---

[21] To be found as a postscript in the book by Thomas Metzinger, Der Ego-Tunnel; Piper, 2014. [Published in English without postscript as 'The Ego Tunnel' by Basic Books, 2009]

a love of truth. He recognizes the consequences of such tendencies, sees the suffering, the misery, the conflicts that result from them, and he hopes that by thoroughly uncovering them, he can open up alternatives and find solutions for such tendencies. On this path he quickly realises that behind the reality produced by "normal" human behaviour and way of being, there must lie hidden another true reality. His greatest concern is to come nearer to this other reality.

One aspect of self-knowledge is of course the recapitulation of the past. As a rule, someone who sets out on the path of self-knowledge will already carry a certain past guilt; confusion and ambiguities that have arisen through long-term 'normal behaviour', through avoidance, repression, splitting-off, etc.. Of course, this also needs to be examined with precision and tidied up, and this is usually a considerable part of the work of self-knowledge. Many people like to take advantage of support for this part. This is called psycho-therapy. If they are lucky, they will find a true therapist who understands psychotherapy as guidance towards self-knowledge. And if not – as long as they are serious – fate will certainly offer them an alternative option, show them another path that they can follow.

However, aside from this restorative work, self-knowledge is something that takes place entirely in the here and now, in the present. And strictly speaking, this also applies to the tidy-up action regarding the personal past and most probably also the collective past. Self-knowledge always happens right now. By looking exactly, seriously and honestly at what is happening now – what is happening within me now or what is going on between us – you stumble across the unfinished aspects of the past, across the old stories that were not consciously experienced. Painstakingly penetrating these old sto-ries with consciousness leads to them being cleansed and thus dissolved, so that eventually all that remains as a task is the moment to moment under-standing of the present. Once an adept of self-knowledge has advanced so far, he has already refined his ability to look sufficiently closely to such an extent that he can be considered a master of his discipline.

So what does an exact method mean – whether applied in creating order with respect to the past or in understanding the present? As soon as this refinement in perception has taken place, it means not missing anything anymore, being actually aware of every blink of the eye. Self-knowledge takes place from moment to moment and in the end there is no longer a moment that does not happen in full awareness of what you are doing and what is going on inside you.

And by that I really mean from moment to moment. The bad habit of occasional awareness resulting in acting out rather than paying close attention at the decisive moment – the moment of anger, of fear, of insult – is widespread among the half-hearted disciples of self-knowledge. Being really awake from moment to moment for an entire lifetime, that is serious self-knowledge.

The refinement of perception is brought about exactly by this precise perception: the gaze is trained by seeing itself. It is an endless process of differentiation of one's perception through perception. No control, no impulse of will, no discipline in the sense of effort and coercion is necessary. It is enough to see. Real seeing leads immediately to insight and understanding, and thus also to new or corrective action. Seeing is understanding, gaining insight and acting.

Awareness, from which attentiveness is born, is enough. It monitors itself, has its own discipline, the discipline of mindfulness, the discipline of love. Awakening for this is enough to set the process of self-knowledge in motion and to drive it forward.

Attentiveness permeates everything not yet perceived in the past and the present with consciousness until the point is reached where all that remains is the easy passage through what is there in the present. This permeation with consciousness dissolves all the past guilt that has accumulated and does not allow any new guilt to be deposited in the present.

How does this dissolving happen?

It is, so to speak, an alchemical transformation process in which the metal lead is converted into gold. The lead is the guilt of the past, the densification of energy that materialized to a certain extent in the body from feelings that were not consciously perceived and worked through. Sluggishness, dullness and apathy alongside possible psychosomatic side effects are the consequences, on which perception can focus in order to awaken the inherent dormant stories.

This awakening, this flooding with consciousness of all that is condensed within, transforms the heaviness into something light. What perception dignifies and liberates from unconsciousness, that is the gold. A wonderful transformation process: everything that has been painfully condensed and hidden in the darkness of unconsciousness becomes transformed through the process of being seen; it transforms itself, by itself, into free, light energy, into which it dissolves. Nothing remains of the past. All that has been retained dies again into the eternal moment, until only the eternal moment and the eternal movement of awareness remain.

At this point, what could be mistaken as the "aim" of self-knowledge – though it is rather an innocent and natural result that emerges from its truthfulness - inevitably becomes apparent.

Just being free of all past guilt and its accompanying fixations and prejudices is a regal state. To be able to go through life as someone liberated, once again as free energy, what a joyful, intelligent state! From within this state it also becomes possible for the adept of self-knowledge to recognize once again this true reality in all its possible unfolding behind the painful reality created by repression of true reality. The blissful state of liberation is its beginning.

Penetrating this true reality with perception, and furthermore with perception from moment to moment, has no end. True reality has an infinite depth. Even if the seeker in addition finally receives the grace to penetrate to the very deepest of everything, to experience the unity of all being, this is only the beginning of an endless journey into a completely new story, a story of truthfulness that is here only just beginning.

Through the refinement that takes place within us as our perception becomes increasingly differentiated by exact moment to moment awareness, we begin to comprehend in progressively more accurate detail the truth and reality that, at first, we could only recognize in rough outline. This is the reason why recapitulation seems for a long time to have no end. Again and again you will have to re-examine the material to illuminate events from another new perspective using the extra light of the increased attentiveness that has been granted to you. Even though at the beginning it may be a matter of crude admission and retraction of denials in relation to past events or what is currently taking place, contemplating the background to what has taken place will nevertheless bring further and more delicate insights to light.

Most importantly, your attention will shift away from your crude reactions to patterns of behaviour and will increasingly focus on the most delicate and subtle thoughts behind them. The thoughts with which you control your life. It will become increasingly clear that it is thinking itself that is the main problem and the main culprit behind all suffering. You will eventually become aware of these ulterior motives in you, especially those present in each and every current moment. You will see that you direct your life with controlling and manipulating thoughts and that this is responsible for all the problems you have. You will also recognize how flawed this is and see that a life directly guided by perception – by seeing – brings a much more joyful existence and lets you enter a reality that lies beyond the suffering of the world.
There is no choice here. You become an outsider in regard to all untruth and everything false. Meditation is the freeing of the mind from all dishonesty, states Krishnamurti in confirmation of the statement by Kant mentioned at the beginning, Meditation is the movement of this honesty in silence. And freedom means infinite space.

May you know yourself, dear friend

Samuel Widmer Nicolet

PS: The next newsletter (13) will be published after mid-January 2017, as we will visit our Indian friends over Christmas/ New Year.

Love Used To Be
(from original lyrics by Jewel, freely interpreted by Samuel)

Love used to be the ruler
From which you measured all
Love used to be the dizzying height
From which you wished to fall
Love used to be the apparition
Towering in your dreams

Love used to be the pyramid
And on top its eye that always sees
Love used to be a sigh
Like petals gently falling down
Love used to be the thirst, oh, and the quenching,
The question in no need of answering

Love used to be hope unflinching
The dare that believed it must
Love used to be the heady feeling
Of flesh heavy with lust
Love used to be a miracle
The proof that God exists

Love used to be the bedrock you built
A life upon into the future reaching
It used to be what woke you each day
And eased me into sleeping
Love used to be our compass
But now we are alone and lost at sea

'Cause love used to be
Love used to be the ruler
From which you measured all
Love used to be
Love used to be
Love used to be

Newsletter 13:
Adaptation, Conformity, Conditioning

January 2017

Dear friend of exact self-knowledge

Unfortunately self-knowledge at the beginning usually brings out unpleasant things for a long time. It is no coincidence that we humans tend to repress much of what we are, and how we behave and think, and even to hide it from ourselves. There is a lot about us that is not very noble at first. It is understandable that we then like to think that we are different, that we prefer to fool ourselves. Often only after a long process does the beauty of our being emerge and for many who embark on this journey, there is no guarantee that they will ever find their way out of the swamp of human misery into the inner beauty of this essence of being.
It therefore takes a great passion for the beauty of the process of self-knowledge per se and a comprehensive perseverance to get to the bottom of the truth. It takes a passionate love for truth to fathom it all.

But finally, if you can mobilise within you this passion and love for truth and an unwavering perseverance towards self-observation, after many setbacks, after much failure, after much frustration, you will reach a critical point where everything changes, after which everything will become easy and truly a joy. For some it will take longer, for others less, but at some point, at least when you are gifted, the human form will fall away from you, as the warriors call this transition.

On the path of self-observation, you gradually and increasingly realise that the key to inner peace is linked to this reacting or not reacting to external and internal challenges. You begin to realise that you constantly split into an observer and an observed, and that this observer rarely agrees with 'what is' and instead always wants everything to be different, continually reacting to everything with rejection or consent. If one day you succeed through insight and increased awareness in silencing this inner commentator that so often becomes entangled in external actions, and succeed in finding an inner calm that accompanies out of compassion of stillness everything happening internally and externally, the human form will one day definitively fall away from you and you will find a home of joyful peace in your relationships beyond that of reaction and counter-reaction. The observer and the observed collapse within you when this human form is lost, or rather the observer ends in you. You no longer respond to every inner or outer challenge, but instead become one with it and let the challenge itself become active within you and find its right action. In this way the mind becomes completely independent of all challenges.

Now one could think that not reacting to anything either positive or negative, letting yourself become a vegetable, would lead you into total adaptation and conformity.

The opposite is the case. Being able to look out of inner stillness empowers you to see unclouded the reality of everything. Nobody can fool you. You see through everything, see it as it is. Because you are no longer forced to react with anger, despair or self-pity, the intelligence of stillness is able to directly deal with the challenge. The challenge itself can become active within you in this stillness and find a solution. You, or rather the stillness within you, are now in direct contact with everything and know how to deal intelligently with everything. It is precisely this action from out of stillness, from the inner centre, that breaks through the wall of adaptation, the facade of the human form in which most people have become entangled.

But before you can discover this inner place, you will probably need to travel a long way along the path of self-exploration. Not that it would take time. On the contrary, once you arrive, you will realise that this state of enlightenment was always immediately accessible. But we humans usually act stupidly. It takes a lot until we can grasp this simplest of the simple and surrender to it. Many different feelings need to be integrated; it is not easy to withdraw all reaction in the face of a challenge and to remain in stillness. It takes a lot of energy. Energy that you gradually build up through your perseverance in the process of self-knowledge.

The many feelings that want to arise in you as a reaction to every inner and outer challenge of life, their layering and endless differentiation that you get to understand by refining your perception and attention, all of this we want to discuss in the coming newsletters.

At first, this narrow inner space of feelings, which excludes and veils us from the real space, from the unlimited space of freedom, appears bewildering, endlessly confusing and chaotic. Only with time, or rather through close observation, does the simple order of these restricting ego states become apparent and through their recognition they begin to lose their power over you.

The first thing that you usually encounter when you set out on the path of self-knowledge is perhaps not an actual feeling, but instead precisely the adaptation of the human form in which the average person has lost himself. It is not actually a state of feeling, but rather the totality of our defence against inner proprioception regarding thoughts and feelings – a bulwark against honest, authentic realness and corresponding relatedness – our amassed resistance against the majority of feelings, which the agreement to conform among people has excluded from our inner repertoire.

This inner breakout from conformity will initially activate all the feelings that you will later need to integrate in inner stillness and retract as unnecessary reactions. You break through the wall of conformity into which you were forced by education, outside influence and shared living. This mainly happens internally, but often, because you do not see it better yet, there is unfortunately also a reaction externally. The path that leads you to being completely devoid of reaction, of which you still have no idea at this point, begins initially with regaining your authentic capacity to react.

Not that conforming is free of reaction. It is strictly maintained and determined by a set of constant inner reactions and ever-the-same rotating wheels of thought. But these reactions are consistently directed against all authentic feelings that want to arise in you and keep them held down and in a state of repression. The newly awakening capability within you to react, however, breaks through precisely this inner frozen layer and frees you for an already slightly larger space of inner freedom.

Self-knowledge is the path. There is no other path that leads to freedom. Yet self-knowledge is also a prison. In just the same way as with conformity, the uninterrupted, accurate, precise self-observation initially strengthens the imprisonment in yourself, in your ego. However, this is not important at the beginning of the process. You won't even notice. Only when you have become so refined in your perception that the loss of human form is within reach, will you realise this. And it is precisely this loss of human form that will lead to this self-centredness of self-knowledge also falling away from you; or rather the process of self-knowledge will lead into a process of meditation, in which the inner stillness that you have found, from now on moves endlessly within the stillness of the Whole. As soon as inner stillness is found and the structure of the ego – the human form, the adapted thought structures of social conformity within you – begins to evaporate, self-knowledge will cease to be an interesting process that has its own beauty, but which also captures you in a narrow space of human imperfection and unpleasantness. Only then does it become a process of freedom in which looking inward and outward is a single, undivided event that reveals, from moment to moment, insight and the wonders of the unity of the essence of being.
But there is still a long way to go, if you are actually at the beginning of the process and not a genius who is catapulted into the freedom of meditation by a single glimpse of recognition.

What do warriors actually understand by this mysterious term when they speak of the human form? We tend to use the word conditioning to describe this and mean the whole pressure of adaptation and conformity to which we are exposed by the respective social conditions, by morality, religion and struggle for life. This pressure, which is passed on to us in the form of rules, laws, upbringing, education and training, forms us into an ego, usually preserving in us a structuring that kills all direct vitality in us or rather encases it in a form. The human form. Our self.
Conditioning and formation of an ego may be indispensable in the development into a human being. Even under the best conditions, even in the most ideal society, we would be subject to conditioning, to ego-formation. In itself, this would be unproblematic. It is natural. In a society that would be aware of this and that would have a keen eye for this process, we would be instructed from childhood on not confusing the ego with our being, with

our actual nature, and instead learn to give it its rightful place as a useful instrument and handle it carefully as with a dangerous tool, fully aware of the danger of its degeneration. We would learn to switch light-footedly between the ego function and our essence, that is, between thinking and the free energy of perception, according to what is required of us in each case.

What makes the conditioning towards a separated ego-conformity so difficult, is the fact that a rotten, depraved society – as we have created it – not only forces us ultimately to the one-sided understanding of ourselves as a separated ego identity, but also additionally blights us from an early age by leading us into competition, envy and possessiveness – and in this context to the suppression of most natural impulses. It forces us into a conforming that serves the power structures within society. It does not want us to be free, authentic human beings, but rather functioning robots for its war, economic and pleasure machinery. It does not want us as independent individuals, but as consumers who depend on it.

Therefore, if we are interested in self-knowledge, then the breaking open of this conditioning must come first, the breaking out from adaptation and conformity, the breaking out from the prison of the ego structure forced upon us – the human form. Freedom must come first. Behind this wall hides all the confusion of feelings: first the defensive feelings and then the rejected feelings, which are initially still childlike and perverted through their oppression. To liberate, understand and finally overcome them is the path of self-knowledge. We must be given the freedom to do so from the outset. This will occupy us in the next newsletters.

The freedom that is additionally brought by exact self-knowledge is the supreme sensitivity and thus the supreme intelligence in which the good can blossom.

May you know yourself, dear friend

Samuel Widmer Nicolet

Last evening the full moon
in play with silver ribbons
and this morning the sun
hidden behind glittering clouds
over a spring landscape
of pastel beauty.
They witness the Great,
from the space of the Real.
But the day was then filled
with the pettiness and turmoil
of mankind
and it compelled one into
the narrowness of its travail.
Only the night
after the evening
full of velvety tones
brought back the peace,
the gaze upon the immense,
the feeling of the essence.
Now in her darkness wafts again
the connection to the you, to all,
gradually once more the state of oneness
drifts into the light of still consciousness.

Dear friends

The news of Samuel's death may well have reached you.... On Wednesday, January 18, 2017, as night became day, as a new morning slowly announced itself, Samuel's heart stopped beating. Now for us nothing is as it was anymore... and yet, in the Great and in the movement for which we have been going together for 30 years, nothing changes!

Samuel's newsletters still continue... His sense of responsibility for us, for what we share, is also reflected in it – what happiness, what a joy, even in this challenging time! As a farewell gift to us, so to speak, he left behind several newsletters.

So that the fire that he was and has kindled in us may not be extinguished and so that we may continue to blossom and to love!

Silent greetings full of gratitude

Danièle Nicolet Widmer

DEFENCE, RESISTANCE, OBSTINACY AND FEAR

February 2017

Dear friend of true self-knowledge,

Self-knowledge is so fascinating because it will explain the entire world to you as part of the truthful recognition of yourself. Whether you study an atom, an elementary particle or even a quark, or whether you look at a social system or attempt to understand an individual human being or some part of nature, you will always be confronted with the basic characteristics and principles that apply throughout the universe. As soon as you study in detail an aspect or a part without isolating it from the whole, you will very quickly recognise that everything is connected, that nothing can be divided and the fact that everything follows the same call. So why not start with yourself?

With regard to exploring self-knowledge, our last newsletter dealt with breaking away from conformity and compliance. Such a breaking out should not really take place externally as this would be merely a reaction and thus keep us entangled in what we want to break away from. It seems likely and most probably inevitable that we will initially make this mistake, thinking that we can free ourselves from what is wrong and what we want to shake off through opposition. But ultimately we will come to realise that freedom only arises by understanding the prison we are in and that its walls can only be torn down by seeing and not by rebelling against it. This is why we will have to start by recapitulating precisely these reactions of defence and resistance that go hand in hand with the awakening for what society and morals have done to us in order to be able to advance on our path of revealing the Innermost in us.

Freeing ourselves, which means totally rejecting society's morals and values, is the first step in the process of self-knowledge. As we have seen in the last newsletter, the freedom to look at everything without any taboos must be there right from the beginning. Only negation of all the thought constructs, to which we are exposed, will enable self-knowledge and meditation. However, freedom comes only from seeing, from detaching ourselves from anything that has been imposed on us, by recognising the personal pool of egoism, into which all of humanity has isolated itself as a result of the conditioning it has experienced, by understanding that we are degenerating in this pool of egoism. By negating what is not love we will find love. In love, the separation between the ego and the Whole disappears, the pool of the ego dissolves itself back into the flow of the Whole.

It is the intelligence of seeing that liberates us from all entanglement. Intelligence is not found in making critical assessments, in judging and being able to differentiate. Seeing what is there indicates intelligence. Really seeing what is there brings about transformation and true change.

Before this can fully prevail in us, we will need to work our way through the individual steps of acquiring self-knowledge, through many errors and through many doubts and failures.

Defence, resistance and defiance against what has been imposed on us will only come alive in us when in the process of self-knowledge we begin to awaken to our conformity with a rotten society and its morbid values such as envy, competition, possessiveness and corruption, and all the conditioning we are subjected to as a result. Since we most likely fail to find immediate access to the essence of this defence, to the rejected feelings (such as powerlessness and defencelessness), we tend to get entangled in defiance based reactions and try to break through the walls of conformity by fighting against them. However, seeing in stillness will soon reveal to us that we are entirely on the wrong path. It will also bring us in contact with the associated fear that the defence would like to avoid.

We begin to surmise, on the one hand, the fear of querulously manoeuvring ourselves into a dead end with associated consequences, and on the other hand, the fear of the essence of rebellion, the rejected feelings, the feelings of exclusion and helplessness. There is also the fear behind conformity and compliance, which we will see later on.

We see that self-knowledge, despite the fact that it has a special kind of beauty in every stage, is not particularly inviting. Who wants to confront feelings such as fear and obstinacy if they can be avoided? It requires the intelligence of insight to keep going and not give up. Not many people seem to have this intelligence.

Liberation from the conditioning we have inevitably experienced, from the bordered-off ego in which we isolate ourselves, is more an elimination of this entire internal inventory, as the warriors call it. We free ourselves from unconscious and habitual submission to these structures of conformity, we accept full responsibility for everything that is there and put aside what we deem not useful. We accept what we believe is still useful, though not as a guide rail to be followed mechanically, rather as vibrant, acknowledged content of our authentic way of being. This is a long process, which everyone of us has to go through at a very individual level. The ego is given its appropriate space, the intellect is relegated to its limited sphere of activity, everything rediscovers its natural and original order. Consequently, it does not make much sense and it is also practically impossible to attempt to describe this process in detail. I will therefore provide just one or two examples for illustration purposes.

Being conditioned to follow traffic rules makes sense, so I will retain it, while being drilled to compete with and compare myself to others I will reject as being destructive and I will therefore delete the associated thought structures within me. Honouring my parents and being grateful to them I recognise, to some extent, as a value that promotes community. Thus I retain these relationships, as something vibrant and alive and not as a habitual pattern, even though in general I avoid any relationships governed merely by custom and tradition and terminate their corresponding patterns in my brain. And so on...

Before this inner order can be revealed as an expression of utmost intelligence, we pass through a complete series of emotional states as part of this process of overcoming compliance and conformity and initially tend to be entangled in them before we understand how to integrate and thus overcome them. As soon as the resistance against the inner truth is waning, our true nature shows itself initially in our animal response options – the defensive feelings such as aggression, anger, hatred, and jealousy with which we often respond to the challenges of reality out of fear. We will look at these defensive feelings next time.

Only when we have freed ourselves through precise observations from all entanglements to which we are bound by these feelings, will the actual feelings, the rejected feelings from which we have tried to escape through these superficial and intense reactions, become visible underneath. Feelings of defencelessness, powerlessness, helplessness as well as abandonment and loneliness will still surround us for a long time afterwards until we finally find peace and inner stillness by surrendering to them. These rejected feelings correspond to a deeper layer of our true nature. They bring us closer to what we will ultimately explore as our Innermost, that what is really true.

Naturally, fear is a dominating factor in this whole matter. In our search for security, we barricade ourselves in our ego, segregate ourselves from all that is unknown and difficult, that might invade us from either inside or outside, adapt to society's demands for conformity, and so on. Fear shows up anywhere on our path to self-knowledge and lurks in the background of all our endeavours. The desire for security, and the fear associated with it, form something like the basic engine behind all those aberrations we humans find ourselves in.

Fear will therefore always accompany us until the end of self-knowledge. It lies behind our intense outbreaks of defensive feelings, in just the same way as it stands in front of our recognition of the feared rejected emotional states. Only when we have worked through all these confusing states in our self-purification process will we be able to fully understand the fear, and only by understanding the ruminating thoughts that drive the fear, will we be able to overcome it or bring it to a stop in us. Freeing ourselves from fear by learning to confront what is there, is one of the main steps on our path to self-knowledge.

Fear is responsible for submission and obedience, creating authority and all the control that goes with it. It is not authority that generates fear – even though in the end there is an interdependency or vicious circle – but vice versa: fear gives rise to the authority, to which it submits in its search for security.

Fear is the actual conditioning factor with which our brain, our mind, conditions itself. Via this conditioning, fear brought forth our society in which we are ultimately trapped. Fear with its negative spin-offs, its servants, the defensive feelings such as envy, hatred, jealousy, greed and ambition, is primarily responsible for the conditioning of our mind and the rotten social system in which our inner state is portrayed. Based on fear, we conform and accept the conditioning of having to be compliant.

Fear wants to avoid the pain that comes with insecurity. Defensive feelings are nothing other than endless filigree excrescences of this fear, just like the rejected feelings are nothing other than the endless differentiations of this pain that we want to avoid. Self-knowledge ultimately opposes this inner disorder and confusion through the discipline of observation and attentiveness with an order that is not its opposite, but rather its end. Something completely new. It brings about clarification through the process of continual learning about yourself, the world, and everything as it happens from moment to moment.

Seeing society as it is, with its aberrations, its derailments, its injustice and monstrosity means recognising oneself. To look at oneself in one's fear driven state, means understanding the society that we are creating through this fear. This "seeing", without any trace of self-pity, defence or judgement, this unemotional and silent observing, ultimately results in freedom from all conditioning, in the freedom of an energy that is not influenced by anything and which we find deep within ourselves. The endlessly destructive cycle of social continuity, in which every generation destroys the next generation, could come to an end.

If many people could discover the path of self-knowledge, then the conditioning and ego-formation that are to some extent inevitable and necessary in certain mechanically functioning areas of everyday life, would no longer degenerate into the evil that destroys everything alive, but would find their place in a grown-up, awakened humanity. Fear and its search for security would be driven back and kept at bay through intelligent and loving guidance, so that the young following the old do not get caught up in the same suffering and do not have to resist the same recurrent imprisonment. The existence of love and compassion, which will single-handedly provide us with security at the end, would make fear largely superfluous.

As we have said at the beginning, self-knowledge will quickly reveal the totality of the basic characteristics and laws that are inherent in everything, the order that applies throughout the universe and each of its parts. It leads you to the oneness of everything, gives you humility to fit into the whole, to find your place in it.

May you follow this call of the Immensity, dear friend.

Samuel Widmer Nicolet

Be again the very special blossom
on the tree of my love,
come back from the valleys
of fear and pain,
and remain the innocent joy,
embellishing my last days.

My heart is yours; not only for you,
but completely for you. Many moons
will it still love you, many suns
still make you happy.
To my heart you are as lovely as May,
like a last springtime granted to us.

Dear readers of Samuel's newsletters

In the process of self-knowledge, as Samuel wrote in this newsletter, energy is released that gives us the freedom to fae death, the unknown that frightens us most.

It has now been more than a month since Samuel - at least as a man of flesh and blood – left our midst. On the one hand, it is only gradually becoming apparent what this really means for us who have shared our whole life with him. On the other hand, you can see what remains as a gift of a great and passionate life and work. The path that we have to take in order to continue and to carry all of this alone, is also gradually becoming apparent to us...

It is wonderful to experience – also in looking back at the last weeks and months – how coherent everything is and to marvel at the brilliant directing of life!

It is particularly comforting to feel and to receive confirmation that a great freedom really does arise from decades of resolute self-knowledge: the freedom to face death. To one person it is the consent to go with it, to the other person the consent to be deprived of the dearest and most important person in life!

Freedom, as Samuel describes it below, is always full of beauty and depth and makes the best of every fate! The freedom that comes from the integration of death carries us greatly and the immense spread between the dimensions brings much magic into our lives!

Of course we are still deeply sad at times... and we do miss Samuel every day in countless situations and moments, but the gratitude for the wonderful life together and for all the incredible gifts he has left behind, lays a golden glow on everything, even in the most difficult moments!

With this in mind, I affectionately greet you through the early spring.

Danièle Nicolet Widmer

March 2017

Dear friends of self-knowledge,

Self-knowledge leads to freedom. But what is freedom? Is it something that you can establish in opposition to something else? Is it something that someone else can gift you? Freedom that depends on someone or something else cannot be freedom. It would leave you castrated. It does not exist in opposition or dependence on something. It stands for itself and knows no opposite. Freedom is an inner state, a space that opens up across all energy centres and emerges when we are not in conflict with anything at all, when we are able to accept everything as it is, when we are able to just be without reacting, when we internally stop the world, which is how the warriors summarise this state. Freedom arises from self-knowledge, the process in which we learn to practice merely pure seeing as an adequate response to everything that happens internally and externally. The freedom to see what is, however, must be there from the beginning so that the great space of freedom can open up in us during the process of seeing. Being able to accept everything as it is does not mean approving everything as it is.

Having looked in our last newsletter at breaking away from conformity and compliance and broken the constricting patterns of this conditioning despite fear and resistance, the next two newsletters will be about facing the defensive feelings that are the first to be set free in us as a result. These feelings are still fully in harmony with the values of our society that is geared toward conformity and compliance. In this society, these defensive feelings such as hatred, jealousy and avarice –the particular focus of this newsletter – are at work, though they operate from the unconscious underground and therefore appear to contradict the superficially stated moral values advocated by this society. Not even a dictator such as Putin dares to be "evil" openly and honestly, even he provides justifications and explanations that are meant to underline his good intentions, though everyone who keeps their eyes open recognises straight away that this is fuelled by nothing else than selfish and ice-cold calculation.

Disclosing these hidden motives and feelings through the process of self-knowledge exposes this duplicity and deceit, which is so commonplace in the egocentric-orientated world, so that it becomes possible to examine the "good and evil". The deceit in our societal moral at least indicates that all human beings, even someone like Putin or Erdogan, have the knowledge deep inside that there is the love of the heart and they have a conscience that immediately shows them the difference between right and wrong. However, since they are not following it, they do not really awaken to the "pure heart" and remain stuck in the lower spheres of the egocentric personality and thus in compliance with the double standards of society. Only by acknowledging the existence of such vicious and devious sentiments such as hatred, jealousy and avarice do we clear the way for the insight of self-knowledge, an awakening for new paths and options and thus for the end of these base motives. Simply said, defensive feelings are an expression of fear, rejected feelings are an aspect of pain or loneliness. The fear that exists is the fear of insecurity, which is represented in us through feelings such as pain and loneliness. Mistakenly, we believe we can find security by suppressing these representatives of insecurity. But naturally, this only increases the chaos and confusion within ourselves and in our world. In the process of self-knowledge, we see through this fallacy and recognise that security – if at all possible – will arise when we give our full attention to precisely these rejected aspects in us, in society, and in the others. When we allow them into our consciousness, wake up to them and integrate them.

The fear and the pain behind it, which is what we actually fear, show themselves in various facets or differentiated types of feelings in our lives. We will look at the most important of these in this and other newsletters, but it will not be possible to acknowledge every aspect. But this is not necessary. It is the task of everyone who is adept at self-knowledge to create an appropriate inventory by recapitulating their own life and achieving a full and comprehensive understanding of all the filigree excrescences of fear and loneliness in themselves. Essentially, the simplified – or superordinate – perspective will be sufficient for us here, namely that we are primarily dealing with fear and pain that must be integrated, and that all other types of feelings can be considered as partial aspects of these main feelings in us.

We would therefore like to turn our attention in this newsletter to three particular defensive feelings or partial aspects of our fear of insecurity. These are hatred, jealousy and avarice, as they are responsible for a lot of misery and disruption in our communal life and form part of the glue that maintains our social conditioning regarding possessiveness, competition and separation.

If obstinacy and resistance solidify our defence into a cooled-down structure of conformity and compliance, we can understand hatred to be the still burning – or rekindled – hot fire of internal rebellion. Like all defensive feelings, this reignited hatred is closer to what is real and alive than the end product of a fully compliant human being. However, due to its confusion and indiscreet nature, hatred is frequently directed at vitality instead of attacking the suppressors of its vitality, and thus it itself becomes evil. Awakening hatred in yourself without acting it out, silently looking at it within yourself, is essential for breaking out of the prison of conformity. Its heat, kept still within, ultimately burns through into the crucible of what is rejected, which then flows into the sea of the Innermost.

Imprisonment is associated with all forms of conformity, all religious beliefs, all ideologies, all forms of membership. Freeing yourself from these forms of imprisonment is a necessary step on the path to freedom. The power of defiance and the heat of hatred, both purified in the stillness of self-knowledge, create the necessary breach in the wall of respectability that oozes deceitfulness. The representatives of this respectability (politicians and functionaries of society, for example) will always be intent on forcing their fellow human beings to function in accordance with the rules of their respectability. But the purified power of defiance and the cleansed heat of hatred will set aside the authority of these rules in favour of love for that what is. This authority of tradition and morality corresponds to cold, frozen hatred, which prevents love and is therefore part of what is evil. Hatred that has come to life again due to self-knowledge, however, is equal to the initial re-germination of love as it begins to direct itself against the suppression of love.

Just as hatred in the service of compliance is responsible for endless suppression and suffering, jealousy in the wake of possessiveness is a major scourge that tries to shackle love. Acted out either unconsciously or consciously, the suppressing (defensive) feelings jointly make up the evil in the world. Understood and redirected in the process of self-knowledge, their energy turns into a weapon against this evil and for love. Hatred and jealousy as aspects of fear attempt to enforce belonging because they are unable to bear the solitude of loneliness. During the process of self-knowledge, we learn to be free from the fear of being an outsider. With the help of the energy that exists in these difficult feelings and that we no longer put into the service of fear, we succeed in shaking ourselves free and liberating ourselves from all dependency regarding belonging. As soon as we stop being jealous, hateful and envious, we become outsiders who no longer run after success or strive for more power or control. Being an outsider then no longer seems like frightening suffering but becomes instead the desired goal of inner understanding. Hatred and jealously fall away from us as soon as we penetrate them with consciousness. The power within them is liberated and placed in the service of love.

We have already referred to the destructive violence of avarice in human interactions in an earlier newsletter. Withholding, avarice, stinginess on all levels of being are among the key manifestations that are born out of fear and inhibit the free flow of energy and love between humans. Avarice is responsible for the hunger and poverty on our planet, for the starvation of the many and the overindulgence of the few. In avarice we can find the condensate of all conformity and the dictatorship of its set of rules. The fact that the ubiquitous avarice – justified everywhere as a sensible attitude to life – is fully suppressed throughout, is its main problem. Waking up to personal avarice, to the frozenness of everything alive deep inside yourself, is an urgent necessity for every student of self-knowledge. Many try to wriggle around it, refuse to admit how totally stingy they are, because they do not want to face the consequence of this insight, which is fair sharing.

In avarice, as in any other feeling, an energy is trapped out of fear, which must be gifted back to life. By recognising that ultimately nothing can be held on to or truly possessed, we learn to reconnect with the insecurity and vulnerability of all that is alive. Admittedly, the fault obviously lies with society, which conditions us in egotistical possessive thinking, from which we are unable to free ourselves. True, it is this corrupt, depraved society that must be changed urgently. However, it will only change when humans, who have created it, renew themselves.

The test question regarding avarice that each individual has to ask himself with honesty, is the following:

Is what I claim and take for myself in a reasonable proportion to what I make available to the common good?

The attempt to definitely possess something will always fail because nothing is permanent in our life. We do not want to experience the emptiness, insecurity, loneliness and the fear that arises from them. This is why we barricade ourselves and why we want to enforce our ego and dominate. This way we entrench ourselves in isolation, in restraint and avarice. In the process of self-knowledge, we let go of all these by recognising their total futility. The energy that is released as a result gives us freedom – the freedom to surrender to death, the unknown, that what scares us the most.

Self-knowledge leads to meditation and ultimately to freedom, the space that emerges when you can finally agree with everything the way it is. Without submitting to what is. Quite the contrary!

In the light of inner stillness, all problems ultimately disappear. It is the light that comes from overcoming all division. From this perspective, everything is okay the way it is. It follows the universal order. As a result, all the difficulties that seem to apply at a less comprehensive level and thus less comprehensive perspective disappear. Stillness is freedom. And freedom arises from recognising the absolute and complete nature of this universal order.

May you find this freedom, dear friend.

Samuel Widmer Nicolet

Notes: Shekar, an Indian friend, has recently translated our book "Living Together" into English[22]. It will be available in a few months. Under the menu item "Community" on our website you will find a few sections and summaries in German and English which deal specifically with community-making.

---

[22] Samuel Widmer Nicolet: Living Together/ Community and Community-Making; Basic-india Editions, 2017

Right now, I am overwhelmed and full of love.
Suddenly the melancholy
that had seized me
has broken open
has given place
to a passion full of surprise.

You have already twice
come to our home.
I was just told,
you came already yesterday.
Now I wait the return of others,
poignant music playing for me,
I feel somehow wistful.

The transience of everything,
especially the beautiful,
the impossibility of exhausting
all love's possibilities,
they sometimes trigger a kind of happiness in me,
which almost hurts and borders on grief.
Wistfulness I call it.

Of all this I send you something,
of bliss, of pain, of passion,
of transience,
of love and sorrow.
May all this touch you,
strike you in the depths.

Dear human beings

It's good to be able to be the loser! It is a fact that again and again – and on a certain level also in principle – we belong to the losers in this world if we go for love, for depth and truth...

Directly in concrete terms and "materially", we have lost the greatest and deepest that we were allowed to get to know on the level of human relatedness, friendship and engagement. How terrible and difficult our lives would be if we were to live with resistance to this loss. We are usually also among the losers in conflicts with the people with whom we live in the village, with professional associations, authorities, politics and the world at large. We belong to those who stand for something that is undesirable, not understood, not loved.

This is probably a good thing as long as the world of winners stands for pleasure, power and egoism!

186

How should we have compassion for all (human) beings, how should we be able to be love, the Whole, and true warriors, if losing, being lost, not having (anymore) and not-receiving is not integrated?

Being the loser – being able to be the loser – frees us, opens us up to the Whole. And if we are the Whole, are we then – in oneness with everything and the intention of the Great – not miraculously winners again? Magical paradox – wonderful life!

Soon the first cherry blossoms will burst open and bring us comforting magic, even if we are among the losers in the human wrangling over competition and power...

As long as there is life on this earth, there will always be a new spring full of innocence – let us look forward to it!

Cherry-blossom-petal-white spring greetings

Danièle Nicolet Widmer

April 2017

Dear friend of self-knowledge,

What is needed in everything you do, including the process of self-knowledge, is passion. And such passion arises when you see a sense of purpose in what you are committed to.

To break through conditioning, you first and foremost need to see it and recognise that you have been conditioned personally, and above all be aware of how and to what you were conditioned. It is not very helpful to think deeply about conditioning. You need to really feel the conditioning in yourself and sense what you have been drilled or trained for. To feel this, to actually perceive it, is already half of the necessary breakthrough. Real recognition takes power away from the patterns of conditioning so that they eventually fall away without difficulty and you can easily detach yourself from them. For example, admitting to myself that I am drilled to be dutiful and unobtrusive, to go through life fearful of my own strength and the authenticity of my own expression, quickly frees me from such or similar patterns of behaviour. You have to develop a great passion for all this if you want to make progress.

The values of our society are based on egotism and possessive thinking, on competition, ambition, envy and greed. All of these are defensive emotional attitudes that hold down and repress our actual feelings such as pain, sorrow and exclusion from consciousness. The average human being lives out of these defensive feelings, out of an egocentric personality that is based on the laws of the two most childlike centres in our energy system and has not yet awakened to the level of the heart. Our society, which is produced by this average human being, is therefore an egocentric society that glorifies division and isolated personal happiness. It still has no idea of common thinking and sharing. There is a lack of passion for shared happiness.

In this and the next newsletter, as in the last one, we want to continue to deal with the defensive feelings and in particular with competition, envy and greed as aspects of our fear of insecurity. These defensive emotions operate from the subconscious of the egocentrically fixated person who has not yet found the maturity of a heart-driven personality.
In the process of self-knowledge it is important to set this maturing process in motion by becoming aware of these subliminal feelings, by assuming full responsibility for them and thereby breaking up the stronghold of conformity, falsehood and double morality, which causes this egocentric fixation on security in individuals and which in society is portrayed as effective morality and tradition.

Competition means comparing yourself, measuring yourself against others. Competition determines our whole life. From an early age we are encouraged and conditioned to compete. The goal is to be better, richer, more beautiful, smarter and stronger than anyone else on all levels. A totally destructive game that inevitably catapults most of us into the position of the loser, from which envy and hatred are born, because we do not think we can bear the exclusion that accompanies it. But even the few winners who succeed in asserting themselves and securing a coveted winner's place are corrupted in the cruel game. Corrupted and obsessed with ambition, they lose all empathy and compassion and are trapped and isolated within themselves, their avarice and their egocentric world. Their greed completely erodes the basis of existence of the people and creatures that populate the earth.
Conditioning for competition is conditioning for division and therefore, as we are not actually divided, for untruth. It is based on a limited optic of division and it cements this division through continuous reinforcement using repetition of the conditioning keywords. Isolation and the flight from its underlying loneliness lead to dependency, which in turn leads to addiction,

to greed for pleasurable things as substitutes, and thus in its wake, the fear of losing them. An endless, destructive vicious circle.

Our society, created by the egocentric spirit of limited thinking, conditioned for division and competition, is full of this destructive game with all its consequences and effects. Justice, fairness, balance, all that for which the falsehood of morality still prides itself, since it cannot completely suppress the conscience of the heart level, is totally disregarded as a result. That human society could ever find its way back to an order of goodness seems absolutely unthinkable, definitely unimaginable, without an Armageddon that would destroy everything beforehand. It seems impossible that mankind will overcome the bulwark of its greed and its avarice through insight.

The good among humans will not come back by us becoming better, as the hypocritical voice of conformity morality dictates, whilst it continues in the underground of consciousness to purposefully provoke division through ambition and competition. Becoming good or becoming better will never bring about the blossoming of the good. Wanting to become good grows out of precisely the same legitimacy that venerates comparison, measurement and evaluation. It is part of the system that is responsible for the domination of that which divides - the evil. Like freedom, being good exists by itself, alone, without an opposite. It takes place now. Where falsehood ends, where evil, envy and competition come to an end, because they are shaken off when we awake to their existence and their dominion over us. To let all that is not good die away, that is the path of self-knowledge. Self-knowledge is dying. Avarice, ambition, envy, competition and greed are expressions of an ego that does not want to die.

Envy and resentment are the natural consequence of a society based on competition. Dissatisfaction, the greed of those left short-changed and those left insatiable, conflict and war are bound to come from it. Problems such as terrorism, for example, will never end with even more control or additional repression. The escalation of 'more-of-it' leads to a war of all against all. To see the justified dissatisfaction behind a phenomenon such as terrorism, to acknowledge the envy that must arise out of injustice alongside the feelings of exclusion and being short-changed that lie beneath, this will be inevitable for humanity. Their intransigence in this respect, the lack of intelligence that lies in not wanting to see what is reality and truth, this will bring about the final showdown.

The freedom to see, to be allowed to look, the freedom to drag the unconscious into the light of consciousness, this must be at the beginning. Because intelligence, an intelligent new look and new beginning, can only become effective where there is freedom.

Greed is misdirected curiosity, the corrupted, originally natural desire for life and the joy of living. It was corrupted by its link to the impact of neglect, the lack of love and care in early childhood. The desire is misdirected by the fact that greed reaches for a substitute and not for the original. Greed is the hunger for life, degenerated into addiction, which has lost its natural orientation and clings to the wrong things without restraint. Desire, the eternal longing for real life, is the innocent life force itself, which gives us meaning and drives us forward. Greed has lost its innocence and, in an unholy alliance with thinking, desiring more and wanting to possess more, it has committed itself to doom.

Revealing the defensive states of envy, competition and greed, of hatred, jealousy and avarice, of violence and counter-violence, is the beginning of a renewal that is urgently required by the individual and the community created by him. And this is what self-knowledge wants to open up in us. However, this first step by itself is not enough. It would be as if a group that wants to engage in community-making were to remain content with being stuck in the early chaos phase. What is needed is the subsequent emptiness phase, a dying produced through insight, where the people in the group give up old ideas, opinions and fixed points of view and are prepared to listen and respond to each other, so that the group can finally find its way to a sense of community that satisfies all.

This process of community-making, which at group level is no different to the process of self-knowledge in individuals, is what humankind will need or would need. It remains a risk that humankind loses itself in the chaos of uncovering conflicts and thereby destroys itself.

After uncovering the defensive feelings that determine us from out of the depths of our consciousness, we also require the discipline of attentiveness, an intelligence of perception that sees that these repressed defensive feelings, despite their power that vehemently wants to be expressed, cannot be acted on. We must learn to keep these feelings still until they release their inner content: the feeling of exclusion and, ultimately beyond that, also the Innermost, the blossoming of goodness and love in us.

In humanity as a whole, we will hardly be able to avoid the fact that "a lot of crockery will be smashed" before we see reason. However, the individuals adept at self-knowledge should be able to find their way directly into the intelligence of stillness and thus into the death of the false and into the deeper layers of our being. In the stillness of meditation, they will free their mind from any dishonesty. What they need is the passion we discussed at the beginning, a passion for self-knowledge and truth, which they find in the attitude and determination of the warrior. In order not to get lost in any blind alleys on the path of self-knowledge, the warrior's tools are needed: taking responsibility, honesty, giving up self-importance, not letting oneself go etc. Only the warrior can truly survive on the path of self-knowledge.

The solution to all human problems, collectively and individually, will not come from uncovering the unsightly truth about defensive feelings. But this is a prerequisite to uncovering even deeper truths. In later newsletters we will primarily deal with the distained rejected feelings of powerlessness, defencelessness and lostness, which only the warrior knows how to quench. It is not only the winner in the deadly game of competitors that is the guilty perpetrator of the misery that has arisen from it. Equally guilty is the loser, who, unable to bear the feelings of exclusion, helplessness and being short-changed, must act out through defensive behaviour.

Not that the loser's silent surrender to the state that is will bring about the solution. On the contrary, the loser's rebellion is required. He must shake off his paralysis, his cowardice and make clear his distress. However, this distress must be recognised and not defensively acted out. Action, from which good blossoms, always comes from out of stillness, from the emptiness that arises from recognition of what is. Pure seeing without reaction is at the same time a direct action. However, it is a direct action that does not create chaos like all reaction that stems from defence against what is, but instead only creates love and joy.

May you discover the fundamental stillness in everything, dear friend

Samuel Widmer Nicolet

The wind visited us
towards dawn,
giving voice to all
that one just wants to forget,
yet also murmuring,
what the heart ever yearns,
recounting the possibilities
of the unthinkable.

Listening to the wind
the desire arose in me,
to stay abed
'til no tiredness remains,
rather mere childlike joy
eager to engage the day.

Is such a thing possible,
that all burden dissolves
back into nothingness
merely through observation?
A day lived out of
innocent curiosity,
a kiss of happiness,
and my love gains wings.

Dear readers of Samuel's newsletters

Often what you need most urgently, is not what you most want.... We don't find the greatest happiness during the most enjoyable and comfortable times, and we don't necessarily feel unhappy in moments of greatest challenge! Is that not so?!

If you live by being and not by doing, then the question of why you have the fate that you have, has become unimportant. It is as it is. And in resting in Oneness, in the life out of abundance, out of the most deep and inexplicable, 'what is' is no longer a consequence of what one is and does. One year the barely open cherry blossoms are swept away by rain and frost; in another year they blossom fully during sunny days and mild nights... and no one questions why it is sometimes this way and another time different!

It is delightful to be at home in this deep space, where the laws of cause and effect no longer apply, but rather life and destiny are an expression of the Great and the Magical, the always right and harmonious – the whole of life becomes a journey through the multiplicity and magnificence of being and creation and is always both wonderful and challenging at the same time – and in any case a great adventure, which is delightful if you can surrender to it without resistance! From this level it makes no sense to divide life and fate into pleasant and unpleasant, right and wrong.

Only up here in the heart-group's forest hut, where I can rest completely alone for two days away from everything of the last three months, did I realize that Samuel wrote the present newsletter last autumn on his last visit to this quiet place... a touching coincidence of life.

Wishing you a peaceful and heartwarming time!

Danièle

May 2017
(drafted in October 2016)

Dear friend of self-knowledge,

It is already cool. But the sun is warming me despite the crisp air. A cleansing barrenness fills the autumn days here in the mountains. It is good to be alone, far from the madness of humans and feel once again the centre of everything. The leaves cast shadows and sway in a light breeze. They form a swell of oneness. The sky is cloudless, now in the evening hours, and so transparently clear. It is quiet despite the cowbells in the distance. And all is still in itself even though there is this motion in everything. One is permeated by order, the sacred order of glorious being.

In this newsletter we will deal one last time within the framework of our examination of self-knowledge with the defensive feelings that first overwhelm us when we venture out of the realm of conditioning, compliance and conformity, and honestly start trying to explore the question "What am I really?" or maybe better "What is it, that actually perceives?".
One defensive emotional attitude plays a particularly important role in this context: pleasure, the human tendency to pursue pleasure and ultimately use it as an essential factor in the defence against a difficult and serious confrontation of issues. This problem – defence through being pleasure-oriented – we will address today in particular, as it is so all-dominant in our world.

Hedonism, the orientation towards pleasure, is the essence of the superficial, frivolous society produced by humans, the essence of their morality or rather immorality. It corresponds to the "way of life", society's lifestyle, indeed its attitude to life, and it is an expression of greed, avarice and competition, the values underlying this society, which we examined in detail on the last few occasions.

It may be that hedonism is inspired by the human penchant for comfort, the nearly invincible laxness of the human condition, as the warriors have called it. Another explanation is certainly the early traumatisation, which most people are exposed to in their childhood, and the pain, which they therefore do not want to experience again later on. Most probably a multi-factor event comes into play here anyway. For us here on the path of acquiring self-knowledge, the causative factors are only of marginal importance. They play merely a subordinate role in overcoming the whole problem. Understanding the causes of something is interesting, but it only brings an intellectual understanding. To overcome a problem requires something quite different, namely the recognition of the problem in all its emotional facets.

Pleasure, what is it?

There is innocent curiosity, the innocent passion and joy of life. Happiness and gaiety. That is not what I mean by pleasure. In innocent happiness, there is not yet any thinking that has taken possession of it or wants to organise it.

Natural happiness and joy of life go together with sensitivity, with receptiveness and touchability. They originate directly from the sensual awareness of the beauty of everything, the immediate openness for everything that can spontaneously delight us.

Pleasure, which is produced by thinking in the attempt to organise innocent happiness, is something quite different. Pleasure takes away the delicacy of sensitivity, dulls us and ultimately makes us unhappy. It is a product of thought that, in turn, like all defensive tendencies, is born out of the fear of and the insecurity in regards to what is truly alive.

Fear, with its anxious thoughts, creates psychological time. It deprives us of the present, the only place in which innocence and thus real joy can show themselves. The fear of not having our needs met, not getting enough, alternates between the future and the past, either believing a past misfortune might be repeated in the future, or a once existing happiness might again be lost in the future.

Fear and pleasure therefore always go hand in hand. What they produce, however, is never happiness and joy of life, but instead endless suffering. The pleasure they create has long lost the ease of real enjoyment and suffers from a severity, an attachment, that leads to endless entanglement and thus to conflict and despair. The dullness that comes upon us reveals itself in the confusion of being no longer able to distinguish between real and unreal, between true and false. The natural intelligence and ability, inherent in the sensitivity of the innocent Now, to directly recognise true and false, has disappeared.

If we look closely at ourselves in the process of self-knowledge, observe how we act, react and respond, we will see that fear arises from thinking, from the conscious and the deeper flowing unconscious thoughts. Fed by the experiences and injuries of the past, or simply by negligence, the fearful thinking tries to avoid repeating the misfortune and to prevent it from happening in the future. However, it overlooks the fact that it thereby ruins everything and manoeuvres itself into a misery, from which it can hardly escape anymore. In the same way, thinking tries to protect itself by attempting to repeat past happiness as pleasure, to keep hold of it and forcibly bring it about again in the future. This, of course, can never succeed, and leads at most to pleasure, this cheap reflection of happiness.

Human society, spoiled and corrupt as it is whether we want to see it or not is based on greed, avarice and competition, and on an immoral attitude that prioritises the pursuit of pleasure above all else. But not the pursuit of happiness. This is, as a rule, taboo and forbid-den: its spontaneity would be much too dangerous and unpredictable for the established power structures that cement the customary rights of this society.

Fear and pleasure bring suffering and hence they produce dependency and addiction as means to escape the suffering. The dependency and addiction are desirable because they can be exploited and they occupy the victims in such a way that they are no longer able to con-front the more serious and deeper issues. Thus, they do not pose a threat to the ruling system.

Real happiness, real joy, spontaneous ecstasy born out of the present are an enrichment; they create no misery. They come and go and leave no trace.

The desire for them is part of our natural, primary and healthy constitution. It is only when thinking comes along, born out of painful experience and sustained by social customs and conditioning, that the vicious circle of anxiety occurs, in which we have lost ourselves. The desire itself, the longing, is a flame within us. A flame of passion and intelligence, capable of penetrating all untruths. It is only when thinking takes possession of this hunger in us, that this pure power is corrupted into a craving for pleasure and it sinks into the stream of suffering that has gripped and dominated all mankind.

In order to be free from this misery, we shall have to free ourselves from the fear, and hence from this secondary kind of supposed happiness, from pleasure. Fear and pleasure are inseparable and belong together. One cannot take them apart. The path of liberation lies in self-knowledge, the intelligent observation and the uncovering of all these interrelations. To enjoy life, to enjoy the beauty of existence, is never the problem, even though the "authorities" of a corrupt world have always wanted to make us believe so. On the contrary, real, very present enjoyment of life is exactly the solution, that which ultimately frees us again and leads us out of painful starvation. However, you will have to put an end to the fear in you, stop wanting to hold on to happiness, forgo security, and accept the ephemeral nature of existence. True life unfolds in freedom, in a freedom for which there are no guarantees.

How can one end this malign mechanism? Is it enough to see how thinking constantly seeks and constantly wants to avoid fear and suffering and to repeat what was pleasurable? Can one really put an end to the suffering that comes from it? Halt the thinking that causes it?
The human mind has adapted itself to suffering. It does not really seek a solution to this misery. It stubbornly and constantly hopes to win the lottery every time, despite the fact that common sense indicates otherwise. It does not see the problem. It seems to be too weak to resist the pull of pleasure, too weak to regain the intelligence of seeing, which it has long since given up.
The human mind has adapted itself to the misery, creating a humanity full of fear and pain, degenerated in a rotten society. That it is suppressing this and simultaneously refusing to believe it does not change anything. Sooner or later the truth invariably catches up. Depression and demise are inevitable.

Is there a solution? Is it enough to face it, to confront it? Do we expect a change on the part of society?

Society will only change if the individual takes new paths. Nobody will solve my problem, unless I do it myself. But if I stand fundamentally renewed in this world, this will be my contribution to the transformation of society.

Does the end of fear, the end of suffering, the solution to this whole drama, come from my own intention to really look, from the persistence to really face it? Will it bring to life an intelligence, a sensitivity and sensibility that will find the solution, that is the solution?

And when I see that pleasure orientation is a fundamentally wrong way of life both for me and for mankind, a way of life from which only misfortune can come, what would then be the right attitude to life?

Can this newly awakened intelligence and newly awakened touchability that comes out of the awakening for the problem and the understanding and penetrating of the problem, linger at the curiosity, the beauty, the happy moment, the moment of joy, without there emerging any thinking that wants to organise this innocence? Can this openness and clarity see the danger that lie within and renounce it? Can this seeing let the happiness of the moment die again at any time, let it go to be ready for what life will bring next? Can a fully developed perception find an innocent ecstasy in this way, in which fear and pleasure cannot arise again?

A pleasure-orientated basic attitude does not only end in an unhappy mankind. It also prevents real happiness as well as the possibility for the space and leisure to emerge, the possibility to pursue the really great questions that mankind will have to answer. It is an additional and endless tragedy that we cannot see that a joyous, common commitment to overcoming poverty and hunger in the world, to a co-existence on equal terms with nature, to a new and fair money system, etc. etc., could be in itself a happiness of compassion that goes far beyond all repetition of shallow pleasure. All the insight we need for it has long been born in mankind. Whether we are thinking of Wilhelm Reich, Karl Marx, Jiddu Krishnamurti, Silvio Gesell, or many, many others, one can clearly see that it is one of the tricks of the forces that want to maintain the status quo at all costs, to quickly and repeatedly present every truth as already failed and obsolete, thereby trying to defuse it.

This brings us to the end of the contemplation of the defensive feelings and internal states that are the first things that we encounter once we start following the path of self-knowledge into our innermost. The defensive feelings and internal states are all aspects or expressions of fear. Of course, there are many other facets to this – stubbornness, complacency, under-handedness, falsehood, domineering behaviour, violence, and distrust, for example –, here we have only looked at the most important of them. Starting with the next newsletter, let us turn to a deeper layer in us, one which ultimately reveals to us self-knowledge. Not yet the innermost truth, we will come to this later, but one which fear and its offshoots, such as greed, avarice and envy, defend against. Anxiety defends against pain, the hurt we do not want. It too appears to us in many facets, of which we also want to consider the most im-portant. Facing the pain, both personal and collective, is the step that lies ahead for humani-ty as a whole. If we pave the way for this step individually, we become pioneers of self-knowledge. The pain and its many extensions, everything that is rejected in us, form the gateway to the innermost, to the sanctuary of innocence, which the adept of self-knowledge seeks.

May you find this sanctuary, dear friend

Samuel Widmer Nicolet

You curiously strange being.
You seemed lost,
when I was with you.
Yet the presentiments of death,
that surrounded you,
seemed inviting to me.
I almost wished it,
to step hand in hand
through this final gate
into the unknown.

Dear women, Dear men, Dear friends

Here comes Samuel's Newsletter 18! I don't have a "preface" for you this time...

I wish you much inspiration through Samuel's words and insights –

Danièle Nicolet Widmer

June 2017

Dear friends of the path of self-knowledge,

In the last newsletter we concluded for the time being our discussion of the defensive feelings: those that are the first to awaken in us as soon as we begin to rattle the structures of conditioning and conformity through self-observation. As promised, in this and the next two newsletters we will deal with the real feelings, those previously suppressed by these fear-controlled defensive states. We call them the rejected or original feelings, those which do not arise as a reaction to another unwanted feeling, but rather occur directly in the life process, triggered by traumatisation and hurt. To be more precise, we should of course add that defensive feelings do not only suppress rejected feelings, they can also suppress other defensive feelings. In the process of self-knowledge, the entire nested ego-structure created by this process has to be dissolved once again layer by layer and illuminated with consciousness. All the states, feelings, reactions and thoughts that we can perceive within us, usually hide something deeper that has been pushed out of our consciousness by defence and dissociation. In the same way as there were defensive feelings such as hate, avarice and jealousy lurking behind a wall of conformity reinforced by fear and defiance, using a precise approach we soon discover those things that these emotions and associated reactions want to suppress and control. And as we have already discovered beforehand, in the end there is even something beautiful hiding behind fear and defiance. While defiance is our latent power that, once liberated, breaks through every wall that constricts us, fear – exposed to the light of choiceless perception – refines itself increasingly into a careful, considered and cautious looking and acting that ultimately originates from seeing reality, from exact self-knowledge. In the light of consciousness, everything finds its way back into the natural pre-existing order that is actually present in the universe.

The purpose of self-knowledge, the purpose of its process of uncovering, is to find the way back to the truth, to the authenticity of one's own experience, and consequently to greater autonomy and quality of life. We thus open ourselves up to a co-operative and intelligent togetherness with all beings that is no longer guided by outdated prejudices. Something true, genuine and deeper lies behind everything that is pretended, false and superficial. In the case of the rejected feelings – such as abandonment, exclusion and feeling short-changed, which we want to examine on this occasion – there are states such as jealousy, hatred and avarice that have literally built up in front of the rejected feelings and have condensed themselves into a barricaded ego so that we no longer have to feel them. Ultimately, the personality trapped in conformity is our imagined ego, which has distanced itself from the frightened being that we want to liberate. Our essence knows no ego. In the end, it once again recognises and risks innocence, a return to the state of innocence, an embedding in an indivisible Whole, whose movement it follows.

The rejected feelings within us have already become much more real, more human, more true; but they are not yet the ultimate truth about us. That we succumb to these rejected feelings relates to our wounded being, which still has to cleanse itself of the traces of its traumatisation before it can rediscover its original innocence and undividedness in the state of meditation. The rejected feelings peel away gradually during the path of self-knowledge and they usually occupy us for a long time until we learn to look behind them and to penetrate even deeper into our true essence. They, too, still represent subtle ego-structures created by the violations of our personal or collective history. They want to be integrated and understood before they finally let the innermost core within us become visible and free.

There is never a real end to this process, since there will always be certain "maintenance work" related to necessary cleansing recapitulation, the restoring of the state of innocence, that will be necessary as part of meditation. A certain amount of past guilt reaccumulates quickly due to friction with all the inconsistencies, especially in the brutal world in which we have to live. But in principle, we finally come in contact with a fundamental source within us that can no longer be questioned, which is beyond all ego-domination and which allows us to feel once again the connection with everything in a true state of undividedness.

But there is still a long way to go. For the time being, we first want to take a closer look at and integrate these softer, finer, but also difficult feelings, which we usually do not really love – otherwise we would not have rejected them throughout the process of ego-development – the rejected or repressed feelings deep inside of us. They will make us softer, more sensitive and more compassionate.

Mostly, however, our resistance against them is very strong, as we do not appreciate their beauty and reject them as unacceptable. The lack of intelligence in this rejection shows our immaturity. Self-knowledge brings us this maturity, this awakening, through which we begin to see the futility of such a strategy of rejection. As we can see from many examples, the world is full of such feelings, even on a large scale, since mankind as a whole is struggling with the needed transition from rejection to acceptance of the things it has rejected. We encounter it in the more than one hundred years of war against drugs, in the current chaos of attempts to control the refugee problem, in the inability to give up obsolete ways of thinking that prevent us from finding new and shared ways of dealing with environmental destruction, the monetary system, creating relationships, the upbringing and education of children, etc. Mankind is suffering from this transition. It will destroy itself if the transition cannot be accomplished.

The path to follow, the path of self-knowledge, consists of sincere and honest looking. This intention alone, this attitude, nullifies any defence. Those who are willing to honestly perceive what is, will also see. Usually not all at once, and unfortunately not immediately and directly. But in a persistent process of true seeing, layers of petals one after another open up until the whole blossom of reality becomes visible in its beauty and incomprehensibility. Since seeing also gives rise to immediate action – initially predominantly internal action, but ultimately also external action – this seeing is enough to change everything, to change us and the world.

We will not be able to look at every single one of the rejected feelings as they dare to come out from under the wilting defensive state that has repressed them for so long. This will be your life's task, dear friend. Something that you will have to accomplish like every single one of us, if you really want to contribute something to a change for the good on earth. And this happens all by itself as soon as you establish in yourself a quality of honesty with regard to your perception.

Here we will turn to the most important rejected feelings and especially those that begin to light up from behind the defensive states we have looked at in the past newsletters: in particular the feelings of abandonment, exclusion, and being short-changed that lie behind jealousy, hate and avarice; the powerlessness, helplessness and defencelessness that lie behind competition, greed and envy, and the loneliness that lies behind our pleasure orientation.

This time, we will address the first three feelings, namely abandonment, exclusion and being short-changed.

When we explore jealousy honestly, we soon discover that abandonment is the feeling from which we want to distance ourselves. However, if we start taking an interest in jealousy and dedicate ourselves to it without prejudice, we discover that in our relationships we are still behaving like babies who do not want to learn to cope on their own. The feeling of shame surrounding this childishly immature attitude that comes over us when we see it, is usually enough to quickly free us from this inability and finally reveal to us the beauty of abandonment, which begins to show itself as soon as the abandonment really has space within us. We will deal with this later when we begin to discover the authentic core within ourselves.

The exclusion, the isolation into which our own hatred has manoeuvred us or that we feel when faced with the hatred of others, is quickly no longer terrifying if we lose our fear of it and decide to live in complete stillness and mindfulness without reacting to it. It is amazing how unproblematic it is to be exposed to feelings of this type and to be able to hold them in oneself, as soon as we give up the idea that this is unacceptable. We experience a real boost in maturity by doing so. From being whining children, who always have to look elsewhere to seek support from others, we transform ourselves into considerate, self-contained adults, who no longer need to react hastily and become entangled in tricky situations as a result. All exploding monsters or addicted fugitives quickly collapse within us and make room for a dignified, intelligent presence that can truly relate to others and does not simply connect with others in predictable, standardised patterns.

What a joy to really grow up! All these rejected states soon turn from being dreaded impositions into best friends – guarantors, who will never let us fall back into the mixed up state of spoiled, hurt infants. An inner order begins to develop. An inner stillness too, an inner space of boundlessness. But we will come to that in later newsletters, once we have come to the end of this supposedly arduous path.

Unfortunately, we humans tend to be endlessly stupid in this process. And it is the same every time. It is only after we have completed a particular step that we realise that we could have done it immediately, without taking any time at all, without endless practice and learning; that there was never any need to stumble into this trap of unintelligently defending ourselves against something that we find challenging, this trap of closing one's eyes to reality and truth. To our excuse it can be argued that this learning step is also a step in our evolutionary development, which hopefully, if many succeed in taking it, will soon be reflected in our genome, and that the stupidity of it, at least in part, corresponds to our current state of consciousness as prescribed by our evolutionary development.

How can we not see that behind the avaricious defensive attitude that excludes us from a generous coexistence, hides our feeling of being shortchanged, which our thinking is afraid could happen again? How can we overlook the stupidity of such a strategy that merely corrupts everything and brings no advantage at all and then stick to it in a narrow-minded manner? How can we not recognise that we are missing out on a shared paradise for as long as we refuse to accept a culture of giving? "Give what you didn't get!" the Buddhists are right-fully teaching. Do they see what beautiful things their forefathers discovered a long time ago? Or do they, too, only move in a tradition of meaningless sayings, barricaded behind ego walls made of hate, avarice, jealousy, fear and resistance, like everyone else?

Why are we never prepared to let an emotion like feeling short-changed spread out within us and experience that this is not so bad, that we are able to do it, and that allowing it is a great liberation? How can we remain so limited, so unenlightened, so unawakened, without at least realising the fact that we have completely lost our way?

Are we ahead of the times, dear friend, in that we have dedicated ourselves to self-knowledge, in that we see that a different path is needed, a different approach to the challenges of life, a new strategy? That we are also willing to attempt this path? Are we the new genome, or do we already carry the new genome within us? This new genome that will finally assert itself, that allows compassion and togetherness and puts it ahead of egoism and egotism, that sees that we can leave behind our fixation on childishness, leave behind the attachment to our animal heritage. That we do not need a dysfunctional, conceited ego based on old injuries in order to master our life? That this ego, on the contrary, keeps our best skills in check? Or are we freaks, exceptional phenomena in a lost world?

In the next newsletter we want to continue to approach our Innermost by illuminating once again the rejected states that are hidden behind defensive behaviours.

May you succeed in being an enlightenment freak, dear friend

Samuel Widmer Nicolet

Left alone, I dream of
what everyone evades.
Hardly comprehensible,
what renders them pale, uplifts me.

Morning is coming and calls the day.
Now leave worries behind,
it wants to lend me,
what night invents but could not do!

Always in secret fate awaits.
It seeks the yours,
the fine and pure,
takes them to its eternal womb.

Yuva, Turkey, July 1st 2017

Dear companions

Today, we have completed our week of Tantra Master Training here in Yuva, north of Izmir in Turkey. Along with about 80 people from Germany and Switzerland, we accepted the invitation of our Turkish friends who want to build a community life here. There are not many places in the world where we are welcome with our work. The fact that we have found another home here to live our deepest passion and carry it into the world makes us very happy!

The fact that so many personal and shared breakthroughs, so much healing, were possible in the past few days, had a lot to do with the fact that before starting the journey the participants had to deal intensively with their fears and resistances against a seminar of this kind in the "Land of Erdogan" and had finally accepted their underlying feelings of helplessness, powerlessness and vulnerability.

So we were able as a group to begin already on this deeper level, which gave us a very joyful and touching gathering. Nourished and encouraged by the "love in the field", by the friendly connections in the world, we will return tomorrow to our home base in Nennigkofen-Lüsslingen...

Tantric-psycholytic-friendly greetings

Danièle Nicolet Widmer

Newsletter 19:
The Rejected Feelings (Powerlessness, Helplessness,
Being at the Mercy of Someone or Something)

July 2017

Dear friend of the path of self-knowledge,

When people set out on the path of self-knowledge, they awaken for it and are at first often enthusiastic and progress rapidly. However, at some point their life theme, which for many people lies in the realm of rejected feelings, catches up with them. They come to a standstill and the breakthrough into the Innermost, which seemed so tangible at the beginning of the process, moves further into the distance again.

Of course, there are also people, in fact the majority, who in connection with their life theme are already at a standstill in the defensive feelings. Jealousy, possessive thinking, need for control, competition and envy, are the 'popular candidates' among the feelings which they simply cannot let go. It is to be expected, however, that the people who are attracted to self-knowledge are those who are already a little more mature and that their main concerns are rather the deeper feelings.

One can only speculate about what makes us more mature or immature in this sense. Obviously, there are differences that can already be observed in children. Even in a family, in which all the children have grown up similarly, there are huge differences. The fact that their learning about the rejected feelings comes to a standstill at the 'stupidest place' in the whole development process is very tragic for the 'more mature' people, as it is extremely exhausting being permanently exposed to the burden of the rejected states. People, who have to struggle with these rejected feelings for a long or endlessly long time, often feel as if they should never have started with self-knowledge as it seems – at least from a superficial point of view – that their fellow human beings, who remain trapped in conformity, are obviously better off. That we have overcome the fear of the deeper layers within us and largely given up the wild reactions of the defensive states, does not protect us from exposure to a great degree of suffering caused by the rejected feelings; to some extent even having to bear all the rejected suffering of humanity.

The task at this point of development is therefore to open oneself up not only to one's personal pain, but also to the stream of suffering of all humanity, to pain itself, supra-individually; in a sense, as preparation for merging into wholeness and unity. This usually also includes coming into contact with the consequences of collective guilt from the distant past and 'being allowed' to clear up one's share of it as a contribution to the Whole. The latter is then already part of the process of encountering the transpersonal boundary layer found at the stillness point in the middle of the head, which prepares our awakening for the very Innermost in us, or in other words, the level of the crown.

As I said before, it is stupid being stuck in this uncomfortable place practically for the rest of our life without ever having the prospect of breaking through. Paradoxically, however, this is precisely the challenge for this section of the path, as we will see in a moment. And it is uncomfortable only insofar as it is not yet possible to find acceptance for this state, and so it seems that only the path of failure leading into despair and depression is open to us.

The confrontation with the liberating rejected feelings is actually a much more interesting and much more demanding challenge to our intelligence than dealing with the agonisingly restrictive defensive states. The crux of the matter is that every rejected feeling in us can only dissolve and gift us the energy freed from it, when we consent to remain with it without complaint, without any defensive reaction, and if and when necessary, forever. This is precisely the paradox: only total acceptance of the unwanted, finally frees us from it.

The prospect of being stranded for the rest of our life with powerlessness, helplessness and being at the mercy of someone or something seems absolutely unacceptable. This is why, in our immaturity, we resist and gladly flee to the defensive feelings that banish this unpleasantness into the underground of our consciousness. However, in our stupidity, we overlook the fact that this cannot provide a solution and that, on the contrary, the unresolved will sooner or later demand its reckoning from us with twice the force.

To surrender, however, seems impossible to us in the beginning. How am I ever supposed to accept that which is simply not acceptable? Only when we break down in despair at this in-solubility does our awakening intelligence begin to realise that the solution lies in this dying – for that is exactly what it is: an act of dying. To be powerless, in a state of powerlessness, is precisely the state we experience at this point, the death point, and it is the state which must be given space in us if the greater things that we want to consider in later writings – love and the destiny that is born of it – can finally pervade us. To be completely helpless, the state of helplessness, is exactly the state of being lost, which finally, once all resistance and reaction have come to an end, can find a home. A total surrender, the state of being at the mercy of everything, which is the prerequisite for us to be accepted into the 'paradise' of stillness.

Our intention in this newsletter was to deal with powerlessness, helplessness and being at the mercy of someone or something. Behind all rejected states we ultimately find an aspect of the essence of our innermost being. The rejected feelings form the entrance to our home, to our core. We will concern ourselves with this much later.
All rejected feelings are repressed by the egocentric personality, by the self of the conforming layer, and repressed further still by the defensive states in the already awakening person. Only when this defensive reaction to our deeper and truer layers of emotions is withdrawn, can the rejected feelings really show themselves in us and blossom fully, so that, to the ex-tent that we can fully integrate them, they can then wither away.
It may be a tragedy not to go beyond this point in a human lifetime. However, to be able to see and accept it as a theme for a lifetime, will be a comfort

to us if this is what has been allotted to us, if these are our limits. The purpose of this – to establish an unbending and unpretentious warrior attitude in us – will undoubtedly gradually reveal itself to us in the years of wrestling with these states, and will, in itself, be a gain worth living for.

Among the defensive feelings we examined, we looked in particular at competition, envy and greed: those states that consciously or mostly unconsciously form the values of our corrupted ego society. It is precisely these facets of our anxious defence that we use to ensure that powerlessness, helplessness and being at the mercy of someone or something – the feelings that they repress – do not occur in our lives. On the path of self-knowledge, we finally for the sake of truth and reality allow these feelings to occur, and finally face up to what appears impossible and leading to insanity.

To be defeated in a competitive struggle leaves us with this almost unbearable feeling of powerlessness, which we normally straightaway defend ourselves against through irate internal and external acting out. Thus, conflict and war have no end in the world.
A person who is adept at self-knowledge chooses a more meaningful strategy. He allows that which – seen superficially – means his downfall. He surrenders. He acknowledges the feeling of powerlessness within himself, he befriends it. He realises that the old strategy gives birth to even more powerlessness. He begins to sense that powerlessness wants to lead him into a new dimension, to reconnect him with a paradise that seemed long lost. With the risk that he might be once and for all stranded in this state of powerlessness, because he will not find the ability in himself to go beyond this state, he sets off on his way. He is powerlessness. He takes the place of those powerless in the world and humanity. What he struggles for and what he may not be able to achieve, what powerlessness – like all rejected feelings – teaches him, is inner stillness.

We will hopefully later discover that this dimension of protected wellbeing without suffering actually exists, and that stillness grants us access to it in meditation.
Envy and greed accompany all competitive struggles. The powerless loser tries through mischievous envious intrigue to compensate for the helpless-

ness that comes from not being able to assert himself, so that he can at least prevail to a limited extent by inflicting damage on the opponent. As long as he remains thus entangled, he is going with the fear that is at the centre of all defensive attitudes and emotional states. He is fear-driven. However, practised in self-knowledge, he finally realises that fearful thinking can only give birth to more and more fearful living and he begins to pause. The act of pausing, of being still, leads him into the woe and pain that forms the essence of all that is rejected, of all rejected states and feelings. In the awakening of the intelligence that brings about this pause, this action through non-action, he begins to realise that pain is the gateway to the Innermost, to enlightenment and release from all woe; and that in acknowledging the woe, the woe itself can show its innermost essence, which leads beyond all suffering. And although he sees that there is no guarantee that he will ever be able to achieve this state of complete stillness that is a prerequisite for this kind of transformation, no guarantee that he could ever catch more than a fleeting notion of the happiness beyond, he begins to set off on his path knowing that he has found his life-theme, his vocation, his destiny. He is prepared to accept that it would be enough for him to become at least an unswerving, steadfast warrior on this path. And as with all rejected feelings, he will certainly gain so much maturity in this process that he will be able to understand that enduring these states is not so difficult in the end, is no longer an endurance, but rather a pause for the beauty that they also possess.

The loser in a competitive struggle is completely at the mercy of the insatiable greed of the powerful and victorious. How could he not need to rebel against this unbearable state of being at their mercy? How could he bear this humiliation? Is his only option to grasp greedily and perish in the attempt? Is there nothing left apart from the present day all too common rampage, the terrorist-like self-destruction should he succumb to it? Or does he see that with such behaviour he will only continue to entangle himself – and with him the whole – in feelings of powerlessness, helplessness and being at the mercy of something or someone; and hence will only inflict even more pain and suffering on a troubled humanity? Will he realise that it ultimately needs a strategy completely different from the previous one, one that definitely leaves behind the animalistic and debilitating heritage and patterns of retaliation? Will he see that it needs a black hole in the midst of this turmoil and that he has been called upon and chosen to be this black hole? A cul-de-sac for all these feelings, the anxious defensive feelings and the painful rejected ones? A black abyss of stillness that ingests all, draws everything into itself and unifies it? A black hole in which everything that drifts over its event horizon is destroyed, erased and pulverised?

Ultimately, the love, born of pain in our innermost, is like a black hole that draws in and purifies all that is impure or repugnant, and which ultimately destroys all untruth and non-love. Love is destruction. Love is a black hole that ultimately opens up into a completely new universe, into a new story. And all that has been, all that has passed, pours into this new universe as newly created purified basic energy. But more about this later in further newsletters.

Can we see all this, dear friend? The truth about it? Or do we let ourselves be convinced by philosophers who today want to make us believe that the all-fulfilling Spirit, which wants to take us in and guide us, does not exist? By those who still cannot or do not want to see that this Spirit has already been scientifically confirmed in the quantum field?[23] By those who think that they are allowed to turn their own limitations into law; who think that their lack of competence in finding access to something, constitutes proof that it does not exist.

Castaneda's great Don Juan, who was long ago expelled from their ranks in an attempt to declare him charlatan, described them as warriors who failed due to lack of clarity. Warriors, at least!

What do you think, my friend? Should we not go one step further together and at least fail when faced with the third enemy, power, rather than fail when faced with the second enemy, clarity, as happened to all of those who, like Moses on Mount Sinai, only get to see the promised land from afar, only fleetingly, because they were not granted the possibility of building in one lifetime sufficient stillness as is necessary for enlightenment? An enlighten-ment, whose existence the philosophers deny, but whose possibility they can

---

[23] See for example: Ulrich Warnke: Quantenphilosophie und Interwelt/ Der Zugang zur verborgenen Essenz des menschlichen Wesens; Scorpio Verlag, 2013 [Quantum Philosophy and Interworld/ Access to the Hidden Essence of the Human Being]

at least recognise. And who, in contrast to the aforesaid philosophers who are perhaps merely jealous, exude wisdom at the end of their lives.

What do you think, dear friend, will we at least be blessed with this good fortune?

Samuel Widmer Nicolet

All poetry seems to escape me,
my body I can hardly endure.
Thoughts migrate through my head,
as if a foreign land.

I have lost my centre,
as if there were nothing but nothing,
as if none had ever suffered,
the great woe of full renunciation.

Where leads the path, Brother Reaper asks,
what do you want, there where you are drawn?
What is dark is not simply bitter,
it is by no means what everything flees.

El Hierro, end of July 2017

Dear readers of Samuel's newsletters

When wakefulness is there between people, when powerlessness and loneliness are held and openness and compassion develop out of this, then soft
tones, soft melodies sound from their mouths and their actions are harmonious
and powerful. The energy, which comes from such life and living together,
nestles itself to the soul of all beings and embeds itself painlessly into nature...

...but when powerlessness and loneliness are acted out, repressed or split off,
everything that comes out of it is coarse, loud, sharp-edged and painful for the
ear, body, heart and soul of all beings.

We are currently spending our first family holiday alone, without dad (and
husband) Samuel: first we spent a few days on a canoe trip, sleeping outside
and cooking on an open fire, now we spend another week on a small, quiet
island. A constantly changing sky, wind, lava rock, tannin scented and spicy
vegetation and a lot of wild sea all around.

Also for the children, who are no longer quite children but still not yet adults, a big confrontation: there is no father anymore who provides clarity and order at the right moment, who "speaks with authority" as supplement to the all supporting and all understanding "daily business" of the mother!

Only gradually does it become clear what this means to live alone with three pubescent young people...

... with this powerlessness and loneliness, often not having for the children (the male energy, role model, identification figure, etc.) that which they need.

All the "rejected" feelings, such as deep sadness, homelessness or being left alone, visit you at times, despite – or because of – the paradise in which we are allowed to spend our holidays right now! They want to be held still and carried so that they can dissolve again into stillness, peace and simplicity... and thus into a carried, held, intimate, joyful state of being.

Every human being seriously concerned with himself and the world has to deal with loneliness once in a while: at first perhaps very often, later only occasionally, but it will always be loneliness, or rather the confrontation with it, which will lead you deeper into reality and into a rich, fulfilling life, whatever destiny one has.

I wish you a passionate summer full of self-knowledge and send you warm greetings

Danièle Nicolet Widmer

August 2017

Dear friends of the spiritual movement,

In our exploration of the path of self-knowledge in this newsletter, we come back one last time to the rejected feelings. In later letters we want to turn to specific aspects and transitions within the process of self-knowledge and then finally to our Innermost, which we hope to open up through this venture.

Of course, there are many other emotional facets within the realm of rejected feelings such as despair, sorrow, disappointment, rejection, being not understood, hopelessness, being lost, neediness and many more that would be worth paying our attention to. They are all expressions and offshoots of the pain and woe that people always like to avoid. However, since everyone adept in self-knowledge must anyway walk the entire path in substance and in per-son and cannot rely on the theoretical knowledge of others, it will suffice here to discuss only the most important rejected states in more detail. Within this process, every aspect of this intensive journey will anyway reveal itself to any serious explorer. And the principle behind it, which always remains the same, will also become increasingly clear to them: be-hind every defence and resistance, if we investigate carefully, we always discover repressed states, which in the case of defensive feelings, such as anger and hate, suppress other origi-al rejected feelings, such as sorrow and shame. That these rejected feelings are still responsible for a certain evasion of reality and thus alienate us from our Innermost, is something that we will outline more clearly in a few months' time, when we get to know the core within ourselves.

As previously said, today we want to turn to the deepest feeling in the realm of rejected states: loneliness. On the one hand, because it comprises something equivalent to the ultimate rejected feeling, that which you will eventually encounter in every confrontation with rejected feelings. And on the other hand, because it correlates, as a rejected feeling, with the defensive state of pleasure orientation that we looked at earlier.

Loneliness is the innermost content of all that is rejected, that which we most want to avoid in all our defensive actions, yet whose acceptance ultimately shows a very special beauty. Loneliness is almost pure original pain as it occurs within us when we are hurt, and hence it forms the opening gateway to the ever sacred and whole Innermost, the core of our being.

Pain is as much part of our authentic original nature as the desire or longing that we examined in connection with defensive states (in particular, pleasure orientation). These are not feelings created, influenced or corrupted by fearful thinking. They appear in us by themselves in innocence, and they soon disappear again if we let them be, just as we can see with small children who get hurt. They cry for a moment and then merrily keep on playing.

The problem that self-knowledge ultimately uncovers and overcomes is that all emotional reactions including the to some extent the real feelings that we call the rejected feelings are either created by the thinking that initiates them or are transformed from original pain. Hence we begin to fall out of innocence, which means that the resulting hurt does not immediately 'fade' again, cannot heal again, but is increasingly banished by the thinking into the unconscious, where the original hurt can no longer dissolve itself, but is instead further distorted, manipulated and preserved. Thus, under the guidance of anxious ego-based thinking, innocent and genuine woe first give rise to feelings of a rejected nature such as sorrow and abandonment, and from out of these rejected feelings arise the subsequent defensive states such as self-pity and jealousy, and then from these defensive states arise obstinacy and resistance by means of the power of thought and further rejection and repression of defensive feelings. If these feelings become more dense and subsequently even more armoured, isolated and deposited in the body and if they also succeed in wrapping the initial fear to a large extent in unconscious stupor, we finally have the perverted normal person who is only able to function like a robot, a zombie, in conformity, conditioning and habit.

This whole tragic misguided process is revealed by self-knowledge and reversed by the power of seeing, of pure perception. Misguided because every child in our world a world conditioned to this self-isolated form of existence, to illusionary separation is massively injured by the confrontation with the zombies that educate it and is conditioned anew and pushed in the direction of this kind of conformity. If they were born into a world not based on fearful defence against reality, there would still be a certain ego-formation that would take place. But any pressure to conform would lead in the direction of a functional ego, transparent in its transient nature, which could be abandoned again at any time in favour of the original state of non-separation. Quite apart from the fact that the original pain that induces this ego formation would remain moderate, since the child would not be received by zombies lacking compassion, but by whole compassionate beings.

The original state that self-knowledge helps to restore thus knows little or no feelings and only little fear. A correspondingly loving and paradise-like environment would not encourage the emergence and consolidation of such feelings. Instead it would help to quickly dissolve them every time they arise.

As soon as the person adept at self-knowledge comes into contact once again with the deep loneliness that slumbers in every rejected feeling, the dissolution of his structures of suffering is likely to be imminent. Nevertheless, as we have seen before, many seekers get stuck in this 'most stupid' place, just before the finish line. This may be related to the basic stupidity and ineptness that most of us display throughout the process, or even to a lack of evolutionary maturity. We've already considered all this before. However, perhaps this strong defensive mechanism of pleasure orientation may also play a role here. It ensures that we never definitively break out of the system of conformity, but rather remain at the very least addicts who can continue to be exploited.

The defence mechanism of hedonism, the addiction to pleasure, uses the basic human trait which the warriors, as already mentioned earlier, call the nearly invincible laxness of the human condition. We like to let ourselves go, we love looking for comfort and alternative satisfaction, we are lazy and often prefer not knowing exactly about things. We usually do not pursue self-knowledge seriously. On whatever grounds this may be based, whether founded on evolution or on conditioning, it is only important for us here that there needs to be a counterbalance, which we must develop within us by applying the warrior's attitude.

This is also part of self-knowledge: being concerned about the instruments that are helpful and can support us on our way. As we recall from our previous excursions: warrior training, meditation, community building, Tantra, psycholysis, etc. Those adept at self-knowledge will concern themselves with all these themes in order to escape the abyss of dependency and addiction.

Earlier we talked about love as a black hole that draws in and purifies all that is discordant and inharmonious. Loneliness, if it is not fully integrated, can become another black hole, one that draws us into darkness rather than light. Not taken in full, loneliness does not show us its beauty, will not become our friend, the one who again and again shows and helps us find our way into the light of the Innermost, into love. Not taken in full, it leads us instead into the maelstrom of substitute gratification, into addiction, into the pleasure addiction that forms one of the strongest defensive structures in us and in society, a structure that quickly reintegrates us and subjugates us to the rules of conformity when we get hooked on it.

Taken in full, loneliness becomes one of our most important teachers, the inner voice that shows us where to go, what is appropriate, what is true and what is false. It leads us into aloneness, into blissful aloneness, in which all the qualities of the Innermost that we later want to learn to understand can blossom in us.

It takes a lot of stillness to hear its voice. Loneliness is the primal source that stands before the primal source within us. Repressed, it becomes a destructive force in us that destroys us, but if understood and loved, it supports us again and again.

Loneliness unites within itself all other rejected states such as abandonment, exclusion and being short-changed, such as powerlessness, helplessness and being at the mercy of something or someone. It brings it all to a single point. It is a black hole whichever way we deal with it. If we allow it to devour us because we have surrendered to it completely, we go through the pain of annihilation and thereby renewal. It is an act of dying. If we allow ourselves to drop all our defences against loneliness and thus be drawn beyond its event horizon, it ultimately spits us out into a new story, into a new life, into a paradisiacal world. Loneliness leads us into true being an outsider. It places us outside the corrupt and spoiled humanity that is trapped in the madness of egomania and conformity, and helps us to establish ourselves there. Loneliness will always be with us, it is a faithful friend who will always remind us when we are about to relapse. Integrated in full, it is no longer painful, but rather affectionate like a mistress. It is the love that always stays with us.

Not taken and instead rejected, loneliness becomes just as much a black hole, a maelstrom that truly destroys us and in no way brings renewal. Not integrated and instead rejected, loneliness becomes a demise into dependency and addiction, which can, when present in a milder form, lead those adept at self-knowledge into this stagnation in development, into this 'most stupid' place we have spoken of, where we can remain stranded on the path of self-knowledge.

Not taken in full, loneliness remains an eternal restlessness in us, a circling around ourselves, an endless search for a way out of it. The paradise of the Innermost, the enlightenment, is therefore withheld from us. As a result of this disturbance, thinking can never become completely still and therefore it not only contaminates the loneliness which thus becomes an inner, rejected problem area – but also corrupts the pure flame of desire and longing, of the natural essence behind all striving for pleasure, by luring it in the wrong direction. The desire or longing, which has been distorted or misguided by thinking into hedonistic behaviour, forms for as long as it remains uninfluenced by thinking – a passionate force in us, a flame without smoke, that supports and drives us in our yearning for what is true, noble, real and good. Like loneliness and alongside loneliness, desire and longing strengthen the pull into the black hole of love rather than the illusionary abyss of addiction. Lost in this abyss, even if only a little bit lost – as happens to warriors, who never completely defeat the third enemy, never completely make their power their own, never learn to ride the tiger – we remain stranded in the 'most stupid place'. Trapped in an endless loop of suffering, just outside the gate to paradise: the gate to inner paradise, to enlightenment, as well as to outer paradise, to liberation from the wheel of fate. The paradise to which the gate can only open, when all searching has found its end in arriving, and when the thinking is thus completely silent in the state of meditation.

What do you think, my dear friends? Are you up to the task? Do you want to be up to the task? Does the beauty of this invitation attract you? Does the notion of this beauty that we sometimes get in, for example, psycholytic experiences, in wonderful tantric or communal togetherness, in the gift of a deep relationship of love – does it help us? Does it help us to persevere on the stony path of eternal failure that leads through all the abysses of defensive and rejected feelings? Does it help to maintain the hope that it is actually possible to get from one shore to the other, even if one sometimes loses the overview completely in the fog of emotional aberrations, in the darkness of illusions created by fearful thinking?

May the power of integrated loneliness carry you to the other shore, dear friends

Samuel Widmer Nicolet

How could I meet you,
there, where you do not pause,
mistaking the heart as not apprehensive,
so long as only you please yourself?

The night is immense and drunk with fate,
no whispering to disturb deep rest.
Awake is the spark of consciousness.
Unheard the depth within.

From that which blinds your eye,
with bare hand how can I shade you?
'Tis something great that changes such
and makes from it a bond of love.

Appendix:
What is spirituality?
(and the intellectual honesty of Thomas Metzinger?)

Lecture by Samuel Widmer for the 3rd International Congress 2017 on Spirituality, conducted by Avanti and the TTSU

What is spirituality?
If one were to ask every person here this same question, one would probably get many different and above all vague and unclear answers. There is hardly a term that I use in my vocabulary that is as diffuse, hard to grasp, and unclearly defined as the term spirituality.
Of course, we are referring to an attitude or belief that is related to our insight into the essence of the undivided nature of all things, with the recognition that everything is one and made of love. But we also use the terms Tantra and psycholysis for the same view of life and for the practice of the way of life that compellingly follows as a result.
That is why I was very happy last year to find a book and a person behind it who, in my opinion, is able to present very coherent thoughts on this subject. Even though I might not agree with his entire philosophy in other respects, his statements on the essence of spirituality as outlined in the epilogue to his book, make me agree with a resounding YES and bring a certain degree of precision to the supposed vagueness that usually surrounds this area of life.
I would therefore like to summarise and comment on them here as an introduction to the subject.

Thomas Metzinger, a philosopher and head of the Theoretical Philosophy and Neuroethics Research Centre at the University of Mainz, is considered one of the most distinguished academic philosophers of today. In his book "The Ego Tunnel"[24], he defines spirituality as the opposite of religion. He sees today's widespread spirituality as an essentially epistemic (i.e. directed towards a specific knowledge goal or specific knowledge) attitude of spiritual

---

[24] Thomas Metzinger: The Ego Tunnel/ The Science of the Mind and the Myth of the Self; Little, Basic Books, 2009

persons, – that is to say an attitude directed towards specific knowledge that for the spiritual seeker is to be gained not in theory but through practice. "Spiritual people want to know, not believe," he says. "They are concerned with an experience-based form of knowledge that has to do with inner attention, body experience and the systematic cultivation of certain altered states of consciousness." The content of the knowledge goals is aimed at liberation and enlightenment and is described as a special form of self-knowledge – self-knowledge that is reflexively directed towards one's own consciousness. It is about consciousness itself, the point where the subject-object structure is dissolved and one goes beyond the first-person-perspective.

At the end of the lecture we will talk about Metzinger's attitude towards changed states of consciousness and thus towards psycholysis as a spiritual aid.

He cites the questions that preoccupy spiritual seekers: "Is spiritual practice a method or rather a letting go of all methods? Does it require effort or is it effortless? How can you see real progress? And can one distinguish between spirituality and illusions, delusions and self-deception?" Ethical integrity – the serious pursuit of a pro-social, ethically consistent life-style observed in behaviour – is cited as a criterion for answering these questions. However, from a scientific point of view, there would be little to say about the desired knowledge, that is the content of spirituality's knowledge goals, since it is hard to communicate in words or justify through argument. The meditation practice associated with spirituality thus involves: ethical integrity through self-knowledge, a radical, existential form of liberation through self-knowledge, as well as training and self-improvement.

It is interesting that Thomas Metzinger, as a scientist and academic philosopher, recognises and honours Krishnamurti as one of the greatest non-academic philosophers of the last century. He sees him as an absolute classic philosopher in a potentially new domain of "Theory of Meditation".

Krishnamurti accepted the incorruptibility of the self as the only spirituality. Metzinger also sees incorruptibility as a "semantic core of a truly philosophical concept of secular spirituality", for which he is striving: incorruptibility in relation to the representatives of belief systems who want to bind meditation to any form of theory; also incorruptibility in relation to the purely ideological forms of rationalist reductionism that would prefer to discredit all non-scientific forms of gaining knowledge; but above all else also an incorruptibility in relation to oneself that remains independent of all theories and ideas.

"But what does it mean to be incorruptible, especially not to be corrupt towards oneself?" he asks. Is there such "inner decency", a clearly identifiable spiritual quality of honesty? Because this should form the basis for ethical integrity, which could serve as a criterion for answering the above-mentioned questions.

He defines intellectual honesty as the attitude of not being prepared to "lie to oneself". He associates it with "decency, sincerity and honesty", with "inner decency", and calls it "a conservative way to be truly subversive".

He is convinced that the representatives of organised religions and all theologians lack intellectual honesty. Intellectual honesty, as he understands it, means that one "does not pretend to know something or to be able to know something that one cannot know, but that one nevertheless possesses an unconditional will to truth and knowledge", especially when it comes to knowing oneself.

It is also a question of moral integrity. In spirituality, just as in science, the "ideal of intelligent, rational reasoning" is about "ethics of inner action for the sake of knowledge" with the aim of "increasing spiritual autonomy". Therefore, a spiritual approach cannot be separated from a truly scientific one.

Thus, in connection with spirituality, we like to talk of intuitive science, as C.G. Jung called it at the time, that can only be based on our own experience and its honest appraisal.

In his remarks on spirituality and its connection to intellectual honesty, Metzinger cites Krishnamurti as well as Immanuel Kant, who stated that it is about "the purity of the intention to be honest with oneself". For Kant, intellectual honesty is "the innermost core of morality", "the essence of the will to ethical integrity". He calls it "the idea of moral goodness in all its purity" and reminds us with this statement that "man, as a moral being, is committed to truthfulness towards himself" and that true spirituality has not only a lot to do with science, but also with strict, old-fashioned rationalism, the conservative way of being truly subversive, as Metzinger calls it, and as we have always seen it. In this context, Metzinger also reminds us of Kant's moral concepts, with which he attempted to understand dishonesty. He spoke of "inner lie" and understands it as a "mere lack of conscientiousness".

Metzinger can also rely on Nietzsche, for whom intellectual honesty formed "the conscience behind conscience". Nietzsche sees that "the will to truthfulness in its highest form" allows us to "face the fact that we are radically mortal beings" and to overcome all self-deception in this respect; or in other words, to discard "the delusional and the systematic denial of finiteness" in our self-knowledge.

To differentiate between religion and spirituality, Metzinger refers finally to the philosopher William Kingdon Clifford. With Clifford's help he condemns the classical standpoint of organised religion in contrast to that of spirituality. He sees fideism – the purely religious point of view, based on which it is legitimate to hold on to convictions not only without positive arguments in favour of them, but even in the face of strong counter-arguments – as "refusal of any ethical attitude to internal action", as "lack of inner decency" and thus as a mental illness. This is because fideism is about "deliberate self-deception, systematic wishful thinking or even paranoia". In contrast, Metzinger recognises the honesty of spirituality as a form of "mental health", as "intellectual integrity".

Metzinger writes:

"If one lets oneself go in the complete absence of positive theoretical or practical reasons and allows oneself to simply hold on to a particular belief, then one has already abandoned the whole idea of ethic of inner action. One rejects the project of intellectual honesty, one rejects, at the level of one's own spirit, not only rationality but also morality. Not only does this change one's own opinions and convictions, but also ultimately the person as a whole loses their integrity. And that's what I meant at the beginning by saying that intellectual honesty is what theologians and representatives of all types of organised religion simply cannot have. Perhaps this sentence initially sounded like cheap polemics or provocation for the sake of provocation itself. But it is about a simple and clear factual point, namely the "principle of self-esteem" – which is, that one does not lose one's dignity and spiritual autonomy. Above all, of course, this statement concerns not only the traditional churches, but also a very large part of the so-called "spiritual alternative culture": much of what has emerged in recent decades in Europe and America lost its progressive impulse long ago. Today it only stabilises the status quo, is characterised by infantile complacency and crude forms of intellectual dishonesty. If one is seriously interested in the question of the possibility of secular spirituality, one has to consider all relevant empirical data and all possible counter-arguments. Philosopher William Clifford said in 1877 regarding people who do not do this: "*If someone deliberately avoids reading books and the company of other people who raise critical questions, then this person's life is one long sin against humanity.*"

Metzinger pursues clarification regarding honesty and narrow-mindedness, as understood by followers of belief systems, by honestly asking himself the classical philosophical and spiritual questions "Does God exist?", "Is there life after death?" and "Is there such a thing as enlightenment?" and comes up with the honest answer that we do not and cannot know anything about it. Although I agree with that, I cannot fully agree with his reasoning on these issues. In it he remains too intellectual and too limited for me. I do not think that he can use the fact that someone has not awakened to a deeper vision to justify that this deeper vision does not exist. But we do not want to go into this here. I hope that others will do so in their contributions over time.

Metzinger sees religion as "the deliberate cultivation of a system of delusion", "the dogmatic and fideistic refusal of an ethic of inner action". In contrast, spirituality is for him "the epistemic attitude that is concerned with knowledge". This is why he regards spirituality as the opposite of religion.
To me, however, spirituality is original, genuine religiosity, a religious attitude that goes hand in hand with the fundamental scientific attitude and is based on honest research and the search for knowledge both inside and outside. To see spirituality as the opposite of religion, would for me, create a new duality and division in the unity. For me, spirituality is mysticism and thus the innermost essence of religiosity. Religion as a belief system, as it is understood today, is thus actually a derailment, a disease, that affects this oneness.
Metzinger believes that science, providing it has not already become a religion and slave to fideism, is in harmony with spirituality, since both proceed from the same value concept. Both know "the unconditional desire for

truth – for insight and not belief" and commit themselves to the "ideal of absolute honesty towards oneself".

Like us, Metzinger hopes that something like "secular spirituality" will be able to become prevalent among people in the coming decades or centuries and save us from our impending downfall. The fact that we are "stubbornly acting against better knowledge" on a collective and often also individual level and that, despite the pressure of time, our outdated conditioning simply does not allow us "to act effectively as a community and develop the necessary political will", leads us to failure. Mankind is thus becoming more and more a victim of its own self-deception and simply cannot adequately respond to the great challenges it faces, even though it has an intellectual insight into the expected consequences and also experiences them at the level of personal consciousness. The question arises as to whether humans, in a spiritual attitude of honesty, could find a unifying strategy in the search for the right answer at the level of common action; whether they could succeed in uniting spirituality and science; and whether humanity can be brought together to any extent to achieve a unified rational, reality- and truth-based perspective. Like us, Metzinger is rather pessimistic about this.

As is to be expected with such an optic regarding spirituality and the honesty or incorruptibility on which it is based, Metzinger also supports psycholysis. Among other things regarding substances and the alternative states of consciousness triggered by them, he bemoans that the "vast majority of people who ultimately have to make the political and legal decisions in question [regarding psycholytic substances and their prohibition or approval] unavoidably do not understand to any extent what they are talking about". He also asks whether "we should accept that someone who is looking for valid spiritual or religious experiences – or who just wants to gain a personal impression for themselves – has to break laws and take all the risks associated with unclear dosages, chemical impurities and dangerous constraints" and concludes that "many aspects of our current drug policy are completely arbitrary and ethically untenable."
However, I do not agree with the solution he is proposing regarding the lifting of prohibition. In this respect, he persists with the traditional belief of scientists and people in authority and wants to leave the field to the special-

ists. In my opinion, the shamanistic tradition, which is inextricably linked to true spirituality, belongs back in the hands of humanity, which does not need any mediators in either instance. For it is precisely the creation of such authorities that ultimately leads us away from the healthy path of finding knowledge through spiritual search and towards the sick dogmatism and fideism of established religions (or sciences?).

Prohibition and the war on drugs do not primarily have the function of discouraging people from intoxicating themselves, but above all else serve the purpose of keeping us busy on an insignificant sidetrack, so that we have no energy, or do not feel the desire, to draw the consequences from the spiritual and world-changing rapture of hallucinogens and empathogens.

Of course, the problem with spirituality, as with science, is that these disciplines can also become "religions" in the fideistic or dogmatic sense. The difficulty we have to overcome is revealed in the question: how can each person check their honesty, so that they will not lie to themselves again. I would not completely trust Metzinger in this respect either. But his reference to Krishnamurti's accuracy and incorruptibility should suffice here.

Where I cannot follow Thomas Metzinger and the current trend in the whole of science – and especially in consciousness and mind research as well as in the neurosciences – is the categorical negation of the spirit. There seems to be a division, a misunderstanding, that prevents insight into the reality of the oneness of creation and creator, the oneness of observer and observed, the oneness of the will to self-organisation and the result of self-organisation. I would like to discuss this issue with such intelligent, scientifically educated and sincerely interested people like him so that I can understand what causes the obvious disguising of the truth on this point.

It leaves me perplexed when Thomas Metzinger writes that "we are ego-machines, natural information processing systems that have emerged in the course of biological evolution on this planet. ... Obviously the evolutionary process that created our bodies, our brains and our conscious mind was not a purposeful chain of events. We are gene copiers with the ability to develop conscious self-models and form large societies. ... But there was no intention behind this whole process – it is the result of blind, upward self-organisation". No intention, but upward self-organisation! For me, there is an obvious contradiction. Self-organisation is in itself an aligned and universal intention, a will to survive, to grow, to select the more suitable.

When Metzinger writes that "if the process that created the biological ego machine had been initiated by something like a person [a god], then one would probably have to describe this person as cruel, perhaps even diabolical. Everything looks like we have never been asked whether we want to exist, and we'll never be asked whether we want to die or whether we are ready for it. In particular, we have never been asked whether we want to live with *this* combination of genes and *this* type of body. And finally, we have certainly never been asked whether we want to live with *this* kind of brain including *this* very special kind of consciousness. Actually, it's high time for a rebellion. But everything we know so far points to a conclusion that is simple but difficult for beings with our spiritual structure to accept: evolution has simply happened – without foresight into the future, coincidentally, without plan, without direction and without goal. There is no one to be despised or rebel against – not even ourselves", then I agree with him that there is no division between creator and creation, no person or something similar in the background that would have pushed the whole thing, but I experience it in such a way that he maintains precisely this division and does not know how to overcome it in his thinking. How else would he arrive at wanting to be asked or wanting to complain? If we ourselves are part of this self-organising process, why should we be in conflict with it? Of course, evolution has simply happened. But obviously it is spirit, universal purpose and directed power. But not behind it or outside it, but inherently.

Metzinger talks about the demystification of the self and the world and sees the danger that we will end up being unable to see the magic – that is, love – in our contact with our fellow human beings. "The cat was let out of the bag a long time ago," he concludes. "We are gene copiers, biorobots that have arisen in the course of evolution on a lonely planet in a cold and empty physical universe. We have a brain, but not an immortal soul, and after about seventy years the curtain falls. There will be no life after death, no punishment and no reward, and in the end, each one of us is alone."

Spirit and love seem to be lost once again in today's philosophy and science. No wonder, I think, when all the magic seems to vanish from the mystery that surrounds us and which we are. Is this due to the old authority problem with a creator god, whom we have rightly dethroned and abolished, but where we unfortunately forgot to also bury the conflict with him?

Finally, I would like to give you a summary in the form of aphorisms that I put together for the announcement of our congress on spirituality and psychotherapy. They are intended to list the most important points regarding the question of "What is spirituality?":

1. Spirituality begins in the pelvis.

2. Self-knowledge, on which True Psychotherapy is based, unfolds naturally and of itself into the realm of spirituality, providing it is seriously pursued.

3. Spirituality is an attitude that is concerned with insight into the essence of the inseparability of everything.

4. Spirituality, in contrast to established religion, is original genuine religiosity, an attitude that goes hand in hand with the demands of science and knowledge-oriented self-knowledge (or psychotherapy, as the case may be).

5. Spiritual practice is not a new method, but rather it consists of overcoming all methods.

6. Spiritually-oriented people rely on insight, not faith.

7. If something can still save and reunite us human beings, it will be spiritual science or secularised spirituality.

8. The spiritual attitude strives not only for insight, but also for ethical action based on this insight.

9. Even those who are spiritual die in the end. (or: spirituality does not protect us from death!)

This I want to tell you,
and enquire of your hesitation:
that home is found only in death,
where hearts eternally bind.

Why do you hesitate, do you wish to stay
in this no man's land, where drift
the unredeemed fools of love,
lost, as if never born?

The loneliness of the solely faithful
rejoiced by those who never regret.
They dare, they know no plagues,
and bear, unending without complaint.

Die, my heart, die!
Break open, wide into this silent heaven,
ever more transparent in evening light.
Along with the fire that warms you,
now that it grows chill,
burn, heart, burn.
Let burn all what still writhes and resists,
all what hurts and seems to you too great,
so that this in stillness is carried homeward.

Die, my heart, die!
Be burst open by the cold and loneliness,
by the pain of separation in this world.
Soften until all hardness melts in you
and let yourself enlighten,
until all shadow drains from you,
from every dark corner,
into which you let no one see,
filled with that you do not wish to share.

Fall, my heart, fall!
Fall through all loneliness of all times,
through disappointment without beginning, without end.
Fall through heaviness, through blackness,
even if you feel like their prisoner.
And through the horrors, fall, fall,
which want to cling to you –
Fall through all bases and nets, through rebellion
and through powerlessness, ever deeper, ever deeper.

And then:
Fly, my heart, fly!
You are the near, you are the wide,
the hard, the soft, the cold, the hot,
'til these be divided no more from each other –
You are the whispering of the forest,
the trembling of the branches, the moaning of the trunks...
You are the sea of all tears,
which you touch with tenderness,
the fire that slowly extinguishes,
and the cruelty too of those who exclude you –

Fly, my heart, fly!
Fly far beyond all that is bound,
not yet born, already dead...
Fly over that which seeks and yearns,
what condemns and knows better...
And caress in passing tired hands,
unruly, dark curls, fine silver threads,
intimately turned towards the coming and going,
towards hard hearts... and all the heavens that are there –

Die, my heart, die into the Whole,
fly, my heart, fly home!

Danièle Nicolet Widmer

September 2017

In the forthcoming newsletters, dear friend, in order to meet our aim of out-
lining the path of self-knowledge – which was our intention in this second
part of our discourse – we would like to examine, alongside our look at our
innermost, some specific aspects of the entire theme, without which our
work would not be complete. We expect to discontinue this letter project
next summer.
In this newsletter we want to look at what we have called the death point,
and then in the next newsletter look at the other important transition, the
stillness, power or insanity point as we call it.

An inner map of self-knowledge would be incomplete if it did not include
an exploration of the important stages of life, and in particular death and
birth. Physical birth plays a major role in the process of self-knowledge insofar as the recapitulation that takes place later in life and is necessary for
the process of self-knowledge, often includes the birth and perinatal phase,
since the events and processes from this stage of life have or could have a
crucial effect on the whole of life and the later psychology of an individual.
However, we do not want to go into any depth here. For more detailed information, we would suggest referring to the work of Stanislav Grof[25], who
published excellent research in this field covering the various perinatal phas-

---

[25] Stanislav Grof: Realms of the Human Unconscious/ Observations from LSD Research,
Souvenir Press, 1996

es and other aspects of our development history, which he also summarised in well-founded theory. Here we also want to deal less with death as the culmination of a life – for this I can recommend my book on dying[26] – not least because it belongs to the incomprehensible aspects of our destiny that we can only experience and not really report on. Should we choose not to leave it alone, we can at best only speculate.

However, death and rebirth are also recurring themes in other contexts during the course of a lifetime. Our whole life span seems to revolve around these two key experiences between which life itself extends, so that it does not seem surprising when they also appear again and again in self-knowledge.

As already mentioned, there are principally two transitions in the process of inner unfolding – or rather unfolding of consciousness – that bring about self-knowledge, and it is these two transitions that will confront us. Self-knowledge can be understood as a process of unfolding in which we set out to realise our innermost or true being, to become a whole or completed human being. Such a process must inevitably be accompanied by the appearance and disappearance of certain traits, characteristics and states, which need to occur before an as rounded as possible entity can definitively establish itself over several stages. Just as in external life – for example, where we first present ourselves as pupils, then as students or apprentices and finally as proven experts, and where each of these stages falls away from us again following its perfection – developmental stages emerge in the inner learning or growth process, in which we then have to die again in order to be reborn. The two main transitions, which we have described as death point and stillness point, are, of course, closely related to the defensive and rejected feelings that we have already dealt with, as well as to the core feelings that we are yet to cover. The death point describes the disengagement from the defensive feelings and awakening for the rejected states within us, while the stillness point describes the overcoming of the rejected feelings and the emergence into the core of our being. That these transitions are difficult and associated with a feeling of dying is something that we have already documented in our

---

[26] Samuel Widmer Nicolet: ... der Tod hingegen ist ein Morgen/ Sterben; Basic Editions, 2015 [...But Death is a Morning/ Dying]

discussion of the rejected feelings. At this point it has to be said that the developments, which we describe here in a somewhat linear manner for the sake of better understanding, are in reality much more chaotic, erratic and initially confusing.

In order to understand the dying or rather the rebirth at these transitions, an additional awakening is needed. Self-knowledge – or rather psychotherapy as an introduction to self-knowledge – mainly uses psychological explanations to describe the processes that take place. However, self-knowledge ultimately leads us to meditation and, as we noted a long time ago, thus into the realm of spirituality. Hence, for certain considerations, spiritual concepts are better suited for a comprehensive understanding of what is happening. Up to now, with our depicted layering of the egocentric personality, we have based our understanding more on a psychological model – the layer model – a somewhat horizontal cut through the person. Working from the outside to the inside, we got to know the adaptation layer, the layer of defensive feelings, the layer of rejected feelings, as well as the core. More information and more details, including schematic diagrams, about this layer model[27] can be found in my books.

In order to better understand the transitions between these layers, however, we also need a vertical cut that is no longer through the psychologically explainable personality, but rather more through the spiritual being that we also comprise. Self-knowledge is a process that we can also understand as an awakening of the personality for its essence, an awakening of the psychologically defined and distinct egocentric personality for the spiritually understood, deeply connected, heart personality, or even for the unlimited spiritual essence behind it.

---

[27] In particular:
Samuel Widmer: Listening into the Heart of Things: The Awakening of Love - On MDMA and LSD - The undesired psychotherapy, Basic Editions, 1997
and:
Samuel Widmer Nicolet: Echte Psychotherapie: Ein Lehrbuch/ Anleitung zur Selbsterkenntnis als therapeutischer Prozess/ Eine Psychotherapie für eine neue Zeit; Basic Editions, 2013 [True Psychotherapy: A textbook/ Introduction to self-knowledge as therapeutic process/ A psychotherapy for a new era]

This is also related to physics or rather to a change in perspective as to how we understand physics. According to Newtonian physics we are materially separate from each other, but according to a quantum-physical viewpoint we could rather be understood to be energies that are not really separate from the whole and are instead closely connected to each other, and which ultimately form an indivisible unit.[28]

These energies, which constitute us, are composed of several centres or compartments characterised by a growing awakening of consciousness that are vertically superimposed on each other – pelvis, abdomen, chest, throat, head, and crown – corresponding to the shift in our perception, or rather the assemblage point of our perception, that occurs from the bottom upwards during the process of self-knowledge. The egocentric personality looks at itself and the world mainly from the pelvis and abdomen, the centres of sexuality and will; the heart personality from heart and throat, the centres of love and expression; while the spiritual being primarily operates from the head centre and the crown above the head, the centres of stillness. More detailed and explanatory information about this vertical and spiritual perception of ourselves can also be found in illustrations and diagrams in another book by me[29].

Another already mentioned and very helpful concept from the warrior world of Castaneda's Don Juan, the assemblage point of perception, also plays a role at this point. We have the ability – like everything else I am trying to explain, something that can be experienced and discovered in the process of self-knowledge – to move the point at which our perception of the world is assembled along a band through various spectra, from each of which the world appears to us differently, especially in terms of its themes

---

[28] Ulrich Warnke: Quantenphilosophie und Interwelt/ Der Zugang zur verborgenen Essenz des menschlichen Wesens; Scorpio Verlag, 2013 [Quantum Philosophy and Interworld/ The Access to the Hidden Intelligence of the Human Being]

[29] Samuel Widmer Nicolet: Essenz schauen: Vom Ruhen im Urgrund des Seins/ Die Spiritualität beginnt im Becken: Ein Buch über Freundschaft und Esoterik; Basic Editions, 1998 [Looking at the Essence: About resting as the very base of all being/ Spirituality begins in the pelvis: A book on esoterics and friendship]

and challenges. This is precisely what we learn to master in the process of self-knowledge: the fluid shift of our assemblage point of perception. That is how it could be summed up. Within the human spectrum, it is precisely these centres – sexuality, will, heart, expression, stillness – in which we can assemble and centre our perception with increasing consciousness, i.e. experience the world and ourselves from these different perspectives.

In this energy system that we form, there is a difficult transition, which we call the death point, between the two lowest centres of sexuality and will, which mainly assemble the perception of the egocentric personality, and the heart centre, which together with the throat or expression centre mainly consists of the perception of the awakened heart personality. This transition is difficult because perception in the lower, immature or childlike centres is based on a view of a world in competition and is therefore controlled by the familiar reactions of the defensive emotions.

The transition to the more conscious or more highly developed heart personality takes place precisely because it learns to let go of this kind of emotional reaction and becomes aware of the deeper, rejected feelings which, in their complete acceptance, ultimately constitute the wholeness of love, as we will understand later. It is precisely this letting go of the repressing feelings in favour of the repressed feelings – as we know from the emptiness stage of the community-building process with groups – that triggers the shift of the assemblage point.

We call this transition a death point, because it confronts us with an initial dying, which also reminds us of our transience, the fact that we are merely of a temporary nature.

As we have already noted: if we surrender to the rejected feelings, if we refrain from defensive repressing reactions against them, then we experience it as if it were a process of dying; something against which we at first – perhaps quite naturally – resist and vehemently defend ourselves. In general, shifting the assemblage point always coincides with these feelings of dying, at least for people who are deeply rooted in egocentricity and have difficulty letting go. What it finally brings us, why it makes sense in the end and why it is more mature to let it happen anyway, we discussed earlier in the case of the rejected feelings. It has, as we now see, to do with the shift of the assemblage point of perception to the heart level and the expanded view of the facts and contexts of the world that we gain from it.

The perception of the world from the perspective of the heart is no longer based on competition, but on togetherness. We begin to awaken for the possibility of co-operation, compassion and sympathy. Love is beginning to become an option. The coarseness of the Newtonian view of separate objects begins to give way to a quantum-physical view of being inseparate.

Mankind as a whole is wrestling with this transition. As far as humanity is concerned, the death point and the challenge it presents correspond to a point in evolutionary development. Many people who take a relatively serious interest in self-knowledge are therefore already threatened with failure in this first difficult transition. They scurry around endlessly in front of the loneliness of this death and do not dare to fall through this bottleneck into the black hole. Again and again they avoid, degenerate into the pleasure-orientation that the world of the egocentric personality continuously offers, are unable to build up the discipline of mindfulness, the inner silence that would enable them to take this step.

Whoever succeeds is then a new person, reborn into another world, though still a long way from reaching the end of the journey of self-knowledge and meditation. Since the majority of the people are not to be found there, the person who succeeds has to bear great loneliness.

Enough for now! Next time we will once again deal with the transitions – primarily with the stillness, power or insanity point – and gain further insight into this matter of shifting the assemblage point and becoming conscious. Only then will we be ready to enter the inner sanctuary of ourselves, the core.

May you not fail at the death point, dear friend, and thus lead mankind as a pioneer.

Samuel Widmer Nicolet

Passion

Although not really cleverer than before,
being with you
was fruitful and illuminating once again.
In any case there is peace all around,
as far as you and I are concerned.
Is it not sad,
not knowing all about love?

Being the one who misses someone,
or needs someone, this you avoid, don't you?
You prefer to hand it to others.
My impression: You keep these feelings at bay.
Along with the accompanying
passion, love and compassion.
As if one must be ashamed of love.

Okay, I say, then I take it upon myself:
Then I miss you.
And I want to see what comes from it.
For you I want to be
the missing and the needing.
The passion too that comes from it.

Dear readers

What Samuel expresses in a condensed form is simply incredible and wonder-ful! How could one not awaken and understand – deeply, fundamentally and lastingly!

Yet everyone will probably simply see and understand only that for which they carry within themsleves the maturity – the inner and energetic preparation and precondition!

It remains only to say – with great gratitude in heart for the grace of enlighten-ment – in the words of Samuel: "May you awaken, dear human, dear being!"

With deep gratitude for being connected and allowed to understand

Danièle Nicolet Widmer

NEWSLETTER 22:
THE STILLNESS POINT, POWER POINT AND INSANITY POINT

October 2017

Dear friend,

After discussing the death point in the last newsletter, the transition from the defensive feelings to the rejected feelings between solar plexus and heart, we want in this newsletter to take a vertical view of the head level in our energy system and examine the second important transition: the stillness, power or insanity point. In a horizontal cross section through our personality, in the layer model, this would correspond to the even more difficult transition between the layer of rejected feelings and the core of the personality, the Innermost within us, for which we will then be ready in the next newsletter. As we have already mentioned, it is this transition that becomes a life theme for many spiritual seekers, as they often fail to integrate the rejected feelings to a sufficient extent and are thus unable to build up enough inner stillness and strength to pass through this gate. Even though it is often misconceived as such, they do not necessarily need to see this as a personal failure. This is because, on the one hand, how far one may go along the path of self-knowledge is determined by the power of the Innermost and is only to a limited extent dependent on oneself, and on the other hand, because the training to become an unshakable warrior, which one receives in a lifelong struggle before this gate, already represents a sufficient goal in itself. Quite apart from this, talking about goals with regard to this royal road is in any case questionable.

Nevertheless, as we have seen in the last newsletter, there are at these transitions – the death point and the stillness point – certain stages that mark "goals" achieved in the development being discussed. The development of consciousness takes place in smaller and larger quantum leaps; not surprising in a process whose progress depends essentially on build-up of energy. The integration of every single emotional aspect equals a quantum leap. The energy of each feeling liberated from the unconscious into consciousness contributes to a pillar of consciousness that rises from the bottom up in the energy body. Completion is ultimately determined by the energetic wholeness of a being when this work is completed. Regarding the latter, however, there is no definitive endpoint to the work, since energy can be repeatedly lost in an open system and certain "maintenance work" remains inevitable for the rest of one's life. Especially in old age – the fourth enemy of the warrior after fear, clarity and power – where it becomes a great challenge not to lose again what has been achieved.

In essence, apart from the many small leaps that we know, there are three major leaps in development or three successive enlightenment states, as we also call them.
Once again, it should be noted that we are not just designing models, putting forward concepts and disseminating theories. We are trying to describe reality in such a way that it can be understood by everyone using the practice of self-knowledge in a context of intuitive science. The description, like any description, is not what it tries to describe, but in our case it is certainly not just something imaginary. On the contrary, it follows closely what we observe, fully knowing that someone else would describe the same thing in a different but comparable way.
The first enlightenment, which usually comes to us in all innocence and as yet without too much self-knowledge work, is the pelvic enlightenment, the perception of a first state of perfect oneness stemming from a fully unfolded centre of sexuality. Everything in the universe is sex, everything is one in a single dance of reproduction and worship, ecstasy and giving life – this is the insight at this level. Spirituality begins in the pelvis.

We obtain pelvic enlightenment as a free of charge advance bonus, so to speak. All it takes is a healthy pelvis and an uninhibited lifestyle. It is life's bonus, the invitation for us to start work with a feeling that there could be more to discover.

We speak of a second enlightenment as soon as the pelvic and abdominal centres – sexuality and will – have been cleansed and liberated through the examination of all defensive states and emotions so that the resulting accumulated energy can pass through the death point to reach the heart space of the rejected feelings. The second enlightenment is a dying, a dying into the oneness of the love of the heart, which will only be completed, however, when the last rejected facet has been integrated.

Enlightenment always begins with satori, with a sudden flash, a first inkling, and only evolves over time, when enough energy has been collected, into a "sustainable" arrival in meditation, the possibility of nirvana or moksha. Here too, the gathering of energy, which further builds up the inner light pillar, goes hand in hand with the integration of all rejected feelings and states, which contribute their liberated energy to the perfection of the state of enlightenment.

Actually, all enlightenment is effortlessly and freely available, even at the level of the second and third breakthrough. Hard work is only necessary insofar as we have armour-plated ourselves individually and, above all, collectively against it. Tearing down these walls requires an effort equivalent to that needed for their construction. Conscious awakening or growth could otherwise be effortless. In this sense, the cosmic orgasm with the whole, the pelvic enlightenment, might not be so completely "free of charge" to most of us.

Here and now, however, we want to look at this second major transition in our energy system or rather the third stage of enlightenment, the stillness, power or insanity point. It becomes possible – initially like a flash of lightening, and later as a somewhat more stable experience – at exactly the moment when all rejected feelings are truly accepted and the last loneliness is integrated. As soon as the energy vessel, the energetic body, is sufficiently full, the energy spills out from the centre at the middle of the energetic body and frees itself up into the crown, into what we call the Innermost or spiritual being behind the egocentric and heart personality. We describe what is experienced there as the core feelings that will be discussed in the next newsletter. The complete integration of the rejected states makes it possible for the conscious entity to swing itself into an even higher consciousness, to shift the assemblage point of perception to this higher consciousness and to perceive the Innermost consciously, unfiltered and directly.

At this point, the philosophical question of whether we are even able to perceive reality directly, which has been debated since Kant and is once again much discussed in recent times, becomes clear. Of course, all our perception at the level of the object body goes through the filter of our senses and nervous system and thus arrives in our brain delayed, manipulated and reconstructed as an inner image. In this coarse Newtonian view, we never actually experience reality as the final reality and, fittingly, never directly, but only as an image, as an everyday-compatible reconstruction within our ego-tunnel, as the philosopher Thomas Metzinger has depicted it. However, if we succeed in realizing such a high energy vibration that we are able to enter the quantum field in terms of perception, then the situation is different. And, as we see it, this is precisely what is taking place in the state of meditation as we move our assemblage point of perception to the level of the head, the stillness point and beyond.

Direct perception is definitely not possible at the Newtonian level, which is why we experience reality as a structure created from isolated objects. However, at the quantum level, energy is experienced directly – not primarily through the senses, but rather directly without link to the self – as energy that is self-aware. The experience of oneness is therefore conceivable, an immersion in the sea of purely energetic existence. In this perception, there is no longer an observer who remains separate from the observed. There is only energy that is aware of itself in ecstatic waves. In a certain sense, there is also no longer a conscious entity, no conscious entity at the level of the self, but only consciousness as the basic intelligence of the energy itself. Wanting to capture the phenomena of quantum energy by means of Newton's physics will always be doomed to failure and will only cause confusion.

Today's philosophers and neuroscientists, and also people in general, deny or do not yet recognize this view. There is no clear distinction between when we or science – for example, with scientific imaging techniques – are moving at the Newtonian level, and when other approaches become necessary because we are dealing with quantum phenomena. It is not possible at this point to go into more detail regarding corresponding proof, and this would anyway be beyond my capabilities. It is perhaps worth remembering the fact that it is questionable to dismiss something as non-existent or impossible simply because you cannot access it yourself. Not having found enlightenment, entitles us at most to not unduly claim it and its wisdom. At this point, too, we would like to draw your attention to the book by Ulrich Warnke[30] for a deeper understanding of the issue.

Why do we call this transition in the head of the energy body the stillness point?

Because the arrival, which is made possible by the integration of all that is rejected, puts an end to all searching in us and reveals to us the innermost qualities of all existence. One of its main qualities, which is particularly overwhelming and inseparable from the simultaneously awakening perception of space that takes place at this point, is the absolute stillness in this vastness. This is why it is called the stillness point: the point at which we attain stillness. But why do we also call this point the power point?

Because, as mentioned earlier, the struggle with the warriors' third enemy, with power, is completed in us at this point. Or maybe not! Another quality of this innermost space is the Absolute: the absolute power and authority of the innermost existence of everything. Those who fail to recognize the facts of the situation at this point and through misjudgement identify themselves with this power instead of surrendering to it in stillness and humility, are in danger of failing, of going insane because of this power, and of never understanding exactly what is the power, with which they believe they are playing and whose pawn they have actually become. The last great defeat, the last great failure that can happen to us. This is why this point is called the power point, the place where our attitude to power becomes definitely clear.

However, why do we also call the point in the middle of the energetic head the insanity point?

To confront the Absolute is indeed supreme sublimity. But it takes a lot of purified, well-centred energy to withstand it and not be swept away by it. To be able to hold the energy of all life in oneself requires a purified, cleansed warrior nature. This should have actually been built up by those adept of

---

[30] Ulrich Warnke: Quantenphilosophie und Interwelt/ Der Zugang zur verborgenen Essenz des menschlichen Wesens; Scorpio Verlag, 2013 [Quantum Philosophy and Interworld/ The Access to the Hidden Essence of the Human Being]

self-knowledge who reach this point. Their inner energy pillar should be al-most perfected by now. Nevertheless, it may happen that they do not with-stand this confrontation with the Supreme and drift instead into defensive, explanatory thoughts.

This transition is a form of dying, too. It is a brain death, even more difficult to accept than the heart death at the death point. As the very last thing, even the personal consciousness is taken away from you at this transition. Nothing remains of the personal nature. One is assimilated into a pure Undivided-ness, commonness, Oneness. No thought remains when faced with this kind of death. Inevitably, this mighty energy shatters you into fragments if you don't know how to face it in complete stillness. This is why it is referred to as the insanity point. Temporarily, hopefully, or permanently, you may lapse into insanity, into an attempt to grasp the inexplicable with thought, and thus be devoured by it.

Such an experience may predestine you to speculate about death and what might come after death. The warriors couldn't resist it and offered a very nice concept regarding the death experience. I have discussed it elsewhere.[31] Here we want to resist and humbly stick to the truth, which is that we can-not really know what can only be experienced. This will protect us from the arrogance that could make us vulnerable to the insanity, to which we do not wish to succumb.

In the next letter we want to examine in more detail the Innermost of our-selves, the quantum field, if you like, that eludes Newtonian judgement and explanation.

In this context, it is important for me to point out once again that all the explanations and descriptions, especially in this and the previous newsletter with regard to the special transitions in the energy system, or in the next newsletter concerning the very core of us, must of course be verified and confirmed within themselves by everyone adept at self-knowledge. Spirit-uality is not a matter of faith, it is a matter of knowing, and there is no theoretical or empirical proof like we find in academic science. To be certain

---

[31] For example: Samuel Widmer Nicolet: ... der Tod hingegen ist ein Morgen/ Sterben; Basic Editions, 2015 [...But Death is a Morning/ Dying]

about something, to really understand something, always requires one's own experience, the utmost exactness and honesty with regard to self-knowledge. It needs the attitude of an intuitive scientific nature or, as I would call it, a genuine scientific religiousness or religious scientificness.

May you explore the Innermost of everything, dear friend

Samuel Widmer Nicolet

To know you first time in the city,
distant darling, to where I often travelled
and where so much began,
lets me think of the transience of all.

Of what at the time seemed like new beginning,
today remains hardly a memory.
Of what at the time the world wanted to change,
today remains no longer a desire.

One has grown old.
And yet there is that,
what always remains new.
It is called love.

This is Samuel's second to last letter in his series of newsletters for you, dear explorers and warriors.

He wrote this newsletter as well as the final one, which we will send to you at the beginning of December, in the silence of the Indian Neredu Valley, a few days before his death.

Is this why he told us about the Innermost, the miracle of the connection at the "dream level", even though in terms of logic and the composition of self-knowledge and energetic laws, it was not yet the time?

Did he sense that he should remind us profoundly once again of what is important in life, in being and being together...?

For a long time we have seen that even though on the whole development follows an imperative, ultimately nothing can be skipped, but also that awakening and integration is not always linear.

Time and again, we break through into a larger space and are able to gain insight into the interconnections within. At the same time, there are always things to integrate, things that we believed had been "dealt with" long ago, parts of our own history and of emotional states to understand and resolve in stillness. Life is not controllable and – fortunately – does not adhere to our concepts, even those that have arisen from a lot of insight and vibrant contact with life!

Autumn storms are sweeping around our house, tearing at the red-green wild vines hanging down from the roof and over the windows, winter will be here soon...

Time once again to attend to the Innermost in us, time of stillness, of aloneness.

Last year, Samuel rejoiced in autumn, in the colours and the wind, even in the mist, as if it were the first or the last autumn of his life on earth –

And the "dreaming", the finding oneself beyond all material and temporal boundaries, the traversing of the great stillness and endlessness, that is what unites us, irrespective of whether we are near or far in material terms, whether we are still on this side, whether we are one of those stretched out between the worlds, or those already completely on the other side!

Autumn golden and gold-hearted greetings

Danièle Nicolet Widmer

November 2017
(drafted January 2017)

Dear friends

Actually, it's much too early to sing of the Innermost. There are still too many defensive structures in us that we need to understand and so many rejected feelings to open up before we are ready for it. But in India, in the Neredu Valley where we are currently staying, the innermost mystery is so close. Nothing else seems to be written and philosophized about here but this inner sanctum, which opens up to us in the end as soon as we have built up sufficient energy in the process of self-knowledge. The Samuel Gita[32], which I promised our Indian friends during our last visit here two years ago, and which I have now written and brought back with me, also tells us about this incomprehensible, this quantum sea in our Innermost, which opens itself up to us once we are able to escape from the restricting laws of the Newtonian object-world, or rather the accompanying monopolising structures of our ego-reality, and into an inner reality.

At night, the sea of stars, the quantum sea, is so wide, so immense here! Is it external or internal?

---

[32] Samuel-Shri-Prem-Avinash-Gita: Der Gesang des Begnadeten/ The Song of the Blessed One, von der unendlichen Liebe/ about love infinite , Basic Editions, 2017 (German/ English)

The Innermost. The innermost core within us. The absolute. The indescribable.

Spirituality starts in the pelvis. By dealing with the states and feelings that act from the lower centres, the centres that form the basis of the egocentric personality (the pelvis and solar plexus) and also the centres of the heart personality (the death point, the heart, the throat up to the stillness point in the head), the assemblage point of perception is gradually moved from the pelvis up to the crown by forming a solid pillar of held energy so that the assemblage point is given the freedom to float freely between all centres according to the respective challenge. The conscious entity gains access to all the humanly possible realms of perception within the total consciousness of existence, to the spiritual essence that awaits us beyond our human boundaries, and awakens for the option of a free mobility of the assemblage point not only in the human realm, but also with respect to further movement into the inexpressible beyond the human spectrum, for the unfolding of the wings of perception into the immeasurable.

At the transition point to this indescribable realm of the perceptible, while awakening for the crown of our energy system and for the world and universal view that results from it, we are immersed into what constitutes us deep down and what connects us with the unity of the Whole, to a certain extent at the quantum level. Awakening for that within us that is an inseparable part of this wholeness and great emptiness, for what we have described as a spiritual essence. The eternal questions of self-knowledge – Who am I? Who are you? – are finally answered here. All these wonderful qualities of the Innermost, this is what we really are deep down. As long as we do not find this in us, no feeling of unity, of unmistakable authenticity will be able to develop in us.

The *dreaming*, on which we reported in the second of our newsletters, begins here: the possibility of travelling in the inexplicable, in the immediate being; of perception, which is no longer bound to a mediator such as body, brain or self, which is no longer subject to the laws of Newtonian physics, but moves freely in the quantum or consciousness field after the ego tunnel has been blown up, and can operate freely in it according to the laws of quantum mechanics.

Pure perception eludes memory and description, it knows only the immediate experience. It is not bound to any substrate. The conscious entity itself is the substrate of its perception. In a certain sense, this highest consciousness therefore also eludes (individual) conscious entity. It is therefore only possible to perceive *and* describe its entrance area, the Innermost within us, this transition point in our energy system above the head, which still belongs to what is human, but which also already belongs to what is non-human, to that which goes beyond the human being. The Innermost in ourselves, which begins to open up to us as soon as we have through the process of self-knowledge built up enough energy and purified ourselves sufficiently for this purpose, is the view of the immensity of space that extends beyond our human existence, the view that is permitted to our human conscious entity. Anything that goes beyond this can only be explored by a spark of perception that has detached itself from the human realm – temporarily, as in *dreaming*, or finally, as in the death of a sublime conscious entity – and only explored directly. In this sense, the Innermost is also the entrance area of death, the realm that even people who have near-death experiences can at best merely probe into. Everything that comes after, although completely open and unlocked, remains an unfathomable mystery. To what extent only sublime consciousness, as it finally grows in the process of self-knowledge, can defeat death in this sense, as the warriors claim, and how far consciousness, which does not reach this dimension, is erased back into the Whole, remains to be seen. We have already discussed these speculations elsewhere. At this point it should be emphasized once again that the awakening for a new level of our energy system and for the new view of the reality that this entails always completely encloses and includes that which has passed away. There is no division, no separation, no dividing line. Everything grows naturally from within itself, the unfolding of a flower one corolla after another, as indicated in the symbol of the lotus flower that has come to be used. In its expanded view of the Whole, the level of the crown also confirms the view of the pelvis, the solar plexus and the heart. Our Innermost still knows the joy of sexual ecstasy, but in contrast to the pelvis, it brings it to an even more ultimate blossom in its detachedness. And it also consummates the will with its humility in its service to the Whole, as it does the heart, which it does not want to forget under any circumstances, with its deep compassion. All is one, the same above, as it is below. It is precisely through the eyes of enlightenment that everything seemingly base is given back its holiness, its wholeness.

The Innermost, this entrance area to the "supernatural", to the Nagual, as the warriors call it, no longer knows any feelings. It is pervaded and constituted by qualities, the qualities of absolute perfection. In their absoluteness, they first confront us with the absoluteness of the authority of death, as we have understood while contemplating the stillness point. Only the person who can fully surrender and devote himself, who can submit to and obey what is true – i.e. the person who has abandoned and left behind every problem of power and authority – can enter into it. Only he will be able to confront the force and grandeur of the absolute nature of stillness, vastness, and emptiness coming toward him from there, without becoming entangled in conflict or going insane. For neither conflict nor thought can remain in there. In releasing these last bonds, the person adept at self-knowledge attains the maturity of the perfect human being. He matures to be able to understand perfection as a human possibility and to accept the task that comes from it: to carry henceforth among humankind the possibility of perfection in human coexistence.

The Innermost. The treasure within us, of which we usually do not know anything, which only serious self-knowledge treasure seekers finally discover in themselves.
Even the Innermost, the being human touched by the great mystery, cannot really be described. To the extent possible, we tried to do so in our book "About the Innermost"[33], which we can refer to here. The innermost encompasses all that is noble, beautiful and good, which we can discover in our shared heart and spirit. It is the essence of this shared heart and spirit. The states that seize and shake us as soon as we come into contact with it, are all sublime in nature. Each one of them captures and includes all the others, each one is part of the essence of all the others. The Innermost is unity. It expresses itself in the form of love and compassion. It constitutes home and arriving, it gifts joy and happiness, and it is serenity and stillness with regard to all actions. There is no end to describing its qualities. To name all

---

[33] Samuel Widmer Nicolet, About the Innermost; BasicIndia Editions, 2011

its conceivable virtues is an insufficient honour. It is sacred, it is wholeness and revelation.

It is actually futile to write about it, unless its poetry is able to spread its scent, to awaken the reader for its beauty. That way it might perhaps make sense. Because the description is not what is described and it contains no instruction how to achieve it, no user guide. It cannot be achieved. Grace is experienced by the person to whom it comes, into whom it flows, who is allowed to express it through his life, his existence. It has no purpose, even though it gives meaning to everything.

What is important is the path of self-knowledge that leads us to its gate. For even if the Innermost cannot be attained, we can prepare ourselves for it to take over the leadership in us, to fill us completely, to want to be born through us into the world of humanity. Without its nourishment, the world loses its meaning, its orientation toward the essential and right. Yet it has no commercial value. It is like the heaven is for the earth: unreachable, for nothing, and yet the support for the fathomlessness on which it rests.

The Innermost is the cornucopia of universal intelligence. Selflessness is the essence of this essence. Everything within is always new, being created. Its content in its inevitability is enlightenment. It is death and life at the point where they transition into one another and at their origin. It brings vulnerability, touchability and openness. Immaculate is its essence, innocence and purity are its power. Passion comes from contact with it, and wakefulness. Through simplicity, one is permeated by it. It is pure magic, incomprehensible, that it is there at all; the wonder of belonging to it is unbelievable.

Just as behind every defensive feeling there is a rejected feeling that emerges through consistent application of self-knowledge archaeology, the same is applicable to the rejected feelings: behind each of them lies one of the qualities of the Innermost to which we lost access in the process of ego formation and which is finally revealed again. Just as behind the defensive states (we have looked in particular at jealousy, hatred and avarice, competition, greed and envy, and even pleasure-orientation) we find the concealed rejected feelings (such as abandonment, being excluded, being short-changed, powerlessness, helplessness as well as being at the mercy of someone or something), behind the rejected feelings we find something all the more wonderful as soon as they are understood and the feelings taken: being accepted behind abandonment, a sense of home behind being excluded, abundance behind being short-changed, liberation behind powerlessness, dignity behind help-lessness, being included behind being at the mercy of someone or something, and love behind all loneliness. The Innermost within us blossoms in our ability to accept the totality of all that is rejected; the rejected within us forms the gateway to the lost paradise of the Innermost. Every single rejected feeling forms an entrance that brings back the innocence of being without hurt.

The path is important. For this reason, we will return to the path of self-knowledge for a number of further newsletters, look again at a series of defensive and rejected feelings, and deal with overcoming them or bringing out the essence of them before we decide to finish this newsletter project in a few months' time. However, it is not so much important to describe this path, but rather to walk it. Something that everyone either does for themselves or chooses not to do. This is the invitation of these essays and the invitation for all of us from life itself, from the life that threw us out of the emptiness of the immeasurable and into the world of form.
It may be as many claim that evolution has no goal, that there is no right or wrong, no reward and punishment for what we do here. During the process, however, it becomes obvious to those striving for self-knowledge that we alone decide with our own will whether our personal life becomes a wonder or a horror. Everyone finds their own Last Judgement within themselves, everyone ultimately orientates themselves according to the state, which they themselves materialise in themselves. Whether it is right or wrong to remain entangled in the hell of base feelings or to fly in the heaven of sublime states can be left to the judgement of each individual. And we have known for a long time that evolution has always selected the more useful things in the long run. Whether it or the universal intelligence behind it has set itself this as a goal, as it seems logical to me, or whether all this is pure coincidence, does not need to concern us any longer.

In any case, what happens to all of us is our fate, which ultimately arises from the wonder or horror we set in motion with our will. Conscious of the quantum field and its basic laws, we recognise that in all cases the contribu-tion of our personal life within the Whole will be effective and is not lost. To assist that the wonderful and not the bad will prevail, seems to us definitely a worthwhile goal.

The wonderful thing would be the materialization of a world, born from the Innermost and its qualities rather than from the wrangling of hurt and defence. A wonder would be a cooperative humanity that coexists together out of dignity, out of sublime states such as wisdom, humility, detachedness and trust. The notion that honesty, integrity, truth and brotherliness could rule among us instead of deceit, hypocrisy, lies and betrayal, and that we have this in our own hands, is not only a stunningly magical notion and a challenge that places us in an immense responsibility, but unfortunately also a final despair that the warrior of self-knowledge in his aloneness has to face. We are reliant on each other, totally dependent on each other: it won't work without you. For the consequence of self-knowledge is actually, at least for much of the time spent on its stony path, primarily one of sheer despair; as someone once said at some point in time. Only serenity in the face of the hopelessness of our human condition and the ascension into the ecstasy of the Innermost that accompanies it, will finally put an end to the despair. It remains to be seen whether the Whole will spiritualise itself, whether evolution will take this path and thus find a solution to the problem of conflict that has been present until now in evolution and thus in us. It seems clear to us that it will anyway certainly prevail with its intention. From this perspective, despair and hopelessness will finally find a definite end.

Two hours' drive north from the Indian city of Bengaluru is the stillness of the Neredu valley. It lies open, just like the Innermost. Unobtrusive and monotonous at first glance, it only discloses its loveliness gradually when you look closer. It demands that we engage with it. Its stillness is based on the absence of people and their thoughts, and not on the absence of noise. On the contrary, a hundred windmills on its gentle slopes generate a constant murmuring sound, similar to the far-away surge of the sea. Sometimes louder and sometime quieter, depending on the wind. We call them the gods who protectively rule over our actions. The mill gods. But you can also hear many birds, the crickets, of course, and other animals. Sometimes music and singing from the little temple at the nearby idyllic waterfall. And sometimes also a faraway road or the widely audible hooting of the train. The silence is all-pervasive as long as nobody is there.

Is the Innermost, the universe, the quantum sea external or internal? Or both?

Space and stillness are one here. Until humans come along and disrupt the stillness, split the space into many disjoint spaces with their continual flashes of thought.

We were able to establish a home here for our work. An undisturbed place among all the uncertainty and transience. Serenity in the face of the hopelessness of the human condition, serenity that arises from the ecstasy of the Innermost, is what finally ends the hopelessness it faces.

We named this little valley Neredu after the Neredu tree that stands at the deepest point of the valley.

May you, dear friends of the royal road of self-knowledge, find in yourselves this end to hopelessness, which is the beginning of all that is sacred.

Samuel Widmer Nicolet

Do you think we will reach the heavens,
bring the stars down among us?
Or will we finally as all the others,
disenchanted surrender to the ordinary?

Do you think the special will touch us forever,
and the great will bless us?
Or will the commonplace conquer us,
devour us as they devour everyone?

What do you mean? Is there the sacred and the other?
Do we believe in stupid illusions?
Or are the others the stupid ones,
those without hope, vision and passion?

Dear friends, warriors, meditators and explorers,

So here is Samuel's final letter to you, his final thoughts, insights and the words that he gave "to the world" before he died.

His very last sentences were for those closest to him, for those who shared his everyday life and those who lived and and shared his path over the course of his life.

He was at home when he died, close-by and in his most intimate surroundings... and yet already very much in the Whole and the Vastness –

Is it not once more the extraordinary direction of life, of death, which made the cut right here?!

With the essence, with the most deep, and with the culmination point of everything, one is alone. Signposts, guidance and support no longer help. One encounters only that which one can open up to by oneself, with which one can be completely alone!

We have received all the support we need, everything is there, is given to us – not only from Samuel, but from all those who have shared the deepest with us –

Everything we need as signpost and reference is at our disposal in life and in the universe.

With the deepest reality, which is something completely different from any description of it, you are alone...
If you have the energy, that is the inner stillness and orientation, and if you are able to open up for it and keep yourself empty, it will certainly touch and completely fill you!

I wish you great earnestness and strength in continuing to be an explorer, a loving and compassionate person, and a humble and passionate warrior –

Viva!

Danièle Nicolet Widmer

December 2017

Dear friends of meditation,

Having advanced into the Innermost in our last newsletter, we have actually reached the goal of self-knowledge. What we are as human and energetic beings, we have now examined and understood. As we have seen earlier, the path of self-knowledge ends here. It affords access to the pathless land of meditation, which opens up from the Innermost, from the core within us, into the immensity of the mystery of the universal being. It is at this point that the perception of the adept of self-knowledge definitively detaches from his own self and begins to turn increasingly to the mystery that surrounds him, of which he is a part.

Of course, this detachment from the fixation on one's own self and thus the commencement of meditation had already started long ago. It was with the awakening of the heart, with the awareness of the rejected feelings, that the compassion for everything and everyone began to awaken in the serious seeker. And it is with the complete comprehension of the wonder of one's own energy system through the awakening for the stillness point and crown, that the seeker's exploration of himself is completely at an end.

Of course, he will continue to devote a certain amount of attention to himself, continue to lead his daily life conscientiously in form and matter as an accomplished warrior, and continue regularly to recapitulate in order to keep himself up-to-date as free energy for the unfolding of his wings of perception into the infinite beyond, either in *dreaming* or in the state of meditation. But the space, in which he is at home and which is infinitely larger and more diverse than he is, will be his main focus from now on. With the energy released by self-knowledge that he now possesses, he also has the power to do so. He is no longer caught up in the all-encompassing conditioning of the normal human being, who does not have a grain of energy left for the mystery that is his home.

Nevertheless, in the final letters we intend to write, we will not indulge in singing about this realm of incredibility – the Nagual of the Warriors, the Nirvana of the Enlightened Ones. This would be a fruitless endeavour, and as far as it is possible to say anything about it, we have already done so.[34] Incidentally, it is perhaps better to read a good book on quantum physics anyway.[35]

Instead, what we plan to do is return again to the beginning and re-examine the enormously important process of self-knowledge on the basis of further examples of transformation from the defensive to the rejected feelings and then ultimately to the core states or rather the qualities of the Innermost. Speculating too much about the intangible is done only by fools who shy away from engaging in the work of self-knowledge that is necessary in order to really encounter it. It is much more meaningful to truly understand this royal road and, above all, to really walk it.

Relationship is one of the main chapters in the manual of self-knowledge. One grows in the process of relationship; relationship is the mirror in which one gradually begins to sense one's own reality. Relationship is also, howev-

---

[34] Samuel-Shri-Prem-Avinash-Gita: Der Gesang des Begnadeten/ The Song of the Blessed One, von der unendlichen Liebe/ about love infinite; Basic Editions, 2017 (Germen/ English)

[35] There are contributions on this topic in my books, for example:
- Samuel Widmer Nicolet: Die Wahrheit; Basic Editions, 2010 [The Truth]
- Samuel Widmer Nicolet mit Marianne Principi: ... jedes Lidschlags dir gewahr/ Tantra/ von der Liebe Lebenskunst; Basic Editions, 2016 [... aware of each blink of the eye/ Tantra / a textbook/ about love's art of living]

er, a major factor in the suffering in most people's lives where it fails and, moreover, a haven of joy where it flourishes. For the warrior, especially for the adept of self-knowledge, it becomes the safe anchor in the storm of energies with which he wrestles provided he finds his troop of warriors.

What destroys relationship is the possessive mentality that dominates everything in an egocentric society. Possession, possessing each other in a relationship, possession itself. Every warrior, who is seriously interested in self-knowledge, has to give it up, overcome it, let it go! There is no alternative; without this there is no dying at the death point, no development beyond the egocentric personality. Control must end, the illusion of separation must be overcome. Everything related to "mine" and "yours" must have an end, otherwise there is no awakening for the level of the one heart, no inclusion in the one spirit.

All understanding of jealousy, greed, avarice and the like will not bring about any change unless there is a willingness growing in you to share and to acknowledge oneness with everything. In the process of self-discovery, we find that behind these defensive states lie rejected feelings such as abandonment and the fear of abandonment, such as feeling short-changed and the fear of not getting enough. If these rejected feelings are fully integrated, fully accepted and appreciated, they finally let the qualities of the Innermost that stand behind them shine through: being accepted, being loved, abundance, all the richness and beauty of the innermost being. We have already seen all this.

Frequently, however, diligent individuals adept at self-knowledge wonder why they do not make progress on these issues, even though they seem to have understood everything.

The key is in the solar plexus, in their will. At many points on the path of self-knowledge there is no need for a process, no development necessary; there is instead a simple step, a simple decision, an act of will, an act of submission of the will to the heart.

When awakening for the heart level the will is not discarded, but rather surrendered to the heart piece by piece. It heals itself in the process, purifies itself, becomes strong and healthy. It has the freedom to say no and as consequence to remain outside the gate. It is this freedom that allows the awakening to become a royal act. For the will has also the freedom to say yes, to open the gate and to surrender freely to the guidance of the universal will, which begins to manifest itself in the awakening heart.

Many seekers want to find a way around this step. They act foolish and wait endlessly for "divine" guidance, where one's own determination and willingness is needed. The door won't open for them.

Holding on fast to what one has, not making oneself and what one has received from life as a gift available to others, can be found in all areas of life. Half the world suffers from hunger and poverty as a result. And the other half also suffers from their gluttony and avarice. We understood all this long ago. This problem can be found in the material world, but also in reference to relationships. And especially in regard to sexuality.

You are mine! You shall have no other gods beside me! One holds fast to this paradigm. But this bastion must fall in favour of "we", of togetherness, in favour of cooperation and compassion. Being rich, having much more than you need, is considered a success and is respected in our society. What an atrocity! Shame must awaken in us, when we do not joyfully contribute our surplus to the common good, when we have too much of something. How come there is no joy for us in making the whole thing flourish? How come this is not our greatest joy? Recognition of the problem is certainly needed, but also action, the act of will.

Is it because we often divide seeing and acting? And do we do this because we have carried the feeling of "mine" and "yours", of separation, into relationships and sexuality, where it does not belong? Is this the devil who does not want to surrender?

Recognising conditioning, seeing through the conditioning to find untruth, that is one thing. Putting this insight into practice, really giving up the conditioning, casting it off, that is another thing; but they have to go hand in hand. True seeing always includes both: recognising and acting immediately according to this insight. The two together must become fused into one. Seeing without the appropriate action that follows immediately from it, is merely intellectualisation. The seeing is not complete, not whole. Seeing and acting must be one process that is indivisible.

Not possessing things does not mean walking around in a monk's habit and taking a vow of poverty. This too is just a trick to avoid the real step of consciously wanting to let go. You can live a rich and full life. Not possessing things is an inner attitude. An attitude in which we do not forget that we are transitory beings, that we are only appointed custodians of all that fate has put at our disposal. A willingness to share anytime, anywhere.

In relationships, this means respecting the freedom of others, not interfering in their will and way of life, recognising the monstrosity of wanting to exercise power or control over others in any way. In sexuality in particular, people are frequently quick to adopt a right of control. We were conditioned to have this right. Students of self-knowledge often discuss without inhibition how much one should and would "allow" one's partner in an "open" relationship. As if one had a right to grant or deny another person their freedom! To see the repulsiveness of it and to renounce it is the key here.

This is often lacking. A lot of people get stuck at this point. It requires a great deal of seriousness in self-knowledge. You have to take it extremely seriously. You have to be exact and mercilessly honest. Otherwise, it remains a dishonest, intellectual game; a game that you only play to avoid feeling guilty. And you are definitely guilty unless you are really serious. We owe the universe our joyful willingness to follow its intention.

Without paying this debt, you will not enter the paradise of the Innermost, you will not experience the ecstasy of enlightenment. The ultimate justice: no one gets more of love and ecstasy than he can allow in himself!

In his new novel "The Mountain Shadow"[36], Gregory David Roberts describes our fate as a "tendency field" and equates it with the universe itself. This tendency field – we would call it the universal intention – drives the movement of the Whole, drives evolution, to ever greater complexity. For him, this is an objective criterion for judging good and evil. According to Roberts "anything that strives for more complexity is good. Anything that tends against complexity is evil." He believes that it is our duty to harmonise ourselves with this tendency field, with the universe and its intention. In his view, bringing ourselves in harmony by examining the positive characteristics in ourselves – what we call the opening up of the qualities of the Innermost through self-knowledge – causes the tendency field to respond with energy and affirmation. But as soon as we work against the tendency field by being negative, loveless, unfair, and unconscious of the truth, we weaken

---

[36] Gregory David Roberts: The Mountain Shadow; Abacus, 2015

our connection to this tendency field – the warriors call it the link to the spirit, to the intention of the universe. The consequence of this is inevitably an existential threat, regardless of how wealthy, famous or powerful we are. Self-organisation! No god, no devil! We ourselves include or exclude ourselves, exactly as we want to.

Like us, Roberts sees it as a no longer questionable fact that the positive characteristics – i.e. the qualities of the Innermost – are already laid down in the quantum field, in every single particle; and the same applies to, for example, the tendency field, space and time, matter and gravity.

Whether you are honest and sincere, whether seeing and acting has become one thing in you, whether you have solved this division between acting and a separate thinking that operates for itself, is something that nobody but you can verify. In the long run it will become visible in your way of life, in your everyday life, but in the immediate moment you are alone with it. No one can help you with that. This freedom belongs to you alone with all the consequences it entails.

In relationship and sexuality, in what is vibrant and alive, there is definitely no place for control and possession. They do not correspond to their truth, their reality. Relationship is not something you can make. It happens to us. Sexuality and its joy are gifted to us. Where we actively pursue them, there is no longer joy. What is vibrant and alive is a self-organising process. The invitation is to follow it lightly, to support it and to serve it. We have no right to extract just what we want for ourselves. That we do it anyway spoils our whole being. It corrupts us, leaves us limited like beggars, handicapped like idiots. Everything royal thus disappears from our lives. Awakening for our magical heritage remains alien to us. That is the price we pay, the consequence of our deal. An earth in despair, a humanity in fear.

God and the devil have been created by man in order to avoid confronting the forces of good and evil within himself. We would rather project them outward. God and the devil do not exist. But there is evil. And there is good. Within us. We are responsible for this.

Essentially, we are conceived as potentially good. Our task is to materialise this potential in the world of form. The Innermost of us is the collection of everything good. All energy united in one is the good. The qualities of the

Innermost include all virtues, all beauty, everything sublime that we know: beauty, love, peace, happiness, serenity and stillness. That we have alienated ourselves from this, fallen from the innocence of this Innermost, is our sin, from which we have to heal again, heal ourselves through self-knowledge.

It's easy to forgive us for falling. It is pardonable, no big deal. That we want to hold on to this fallen state, do not want to correct what has to be corrected, want to hold on to possession and control against our better judgement, makes us evil. The fact that we do not want to acknowledge our task posed by the Great Spirit, the task of realising good in the material dimension, is what is evil in us. It excludes us from paradise. We are thus excluding ourselves from paradise. There is no god or devil who sentences us to such a punishment. We do it ourselves.

.And what about interference in relationships when it comes to the question of self-knowledge? Are we not allowed to remind someone else, show him how wrong he is, how lost he is? May we not remind him that he is not doing good? Would this already constitute interference, control, power and the wish to dominate someone?

Of course you may! As long as we leave the other person the freedom to remain stupid, to be evil, to reject, to not to want to look. There is a fine line between pointing something out and wanting to manipulate. Here, too, a lot of self-knowledge is needed, a great deal of integration of the loneliness, which one person leaves behind for the other if he does not want to join what is right, and whose non-integration is ultimately precisely what is responsible for the tendency to exercise power and control. Everyone who has gone far on the path to the Innermost is called upon to be a teacher. Failure to do so would be a refusal. But anyone who wants to be a real teacher will be careful, will be wary of becoming enslaved by the third enemy of the warriors, by power.

For the time being, the Innermost remains a solitary paradise, a mystery in which loneliness will still reside for a long time to come.

May you enjoy this solitude in the state of meditation, dear friends

Samuel Widmer Nicolet

The last hurdle of the day is overcome.
The wind from the east was mighty today.
Icy he crawled under shirt and coat,
and rattled all window panes.
It is expected to become yet colder.
The evening was fine, full-bodied and strewn
with white cherry blossom petals.
Now die into the night
and into the Immeasurable.
Will my love find you there?

POSTSCRIPT

Samuel's intention was to include here an appendix containing all documentation related to the criminal proceedings; documents which on tactical grounds related to the process had not been included as attachments to the newsletters or had been even withheld from public prosecutor Ravicini.

Unfortunately, after more than three years, the criminal proceedings have not yet been concluded. Even after Samuel's death, the public prosecutor's office still seems to be hoping to press charges based on the never proved, slanderous accusations made at the time. We see ourselves therefore compelled at the moment to continue withholding certain information.